CW01497740

Living
the Liturgy

Living the Liturgy

A Witness

NOTES FROM COMMUNITY CONVERSATIONS

LUIGI GIUSSANI

Edited with an introduction by
FRANCESCO BRASCHI

Translated by
MATTHEW HENRY

With the assistance of
LAURA FERRARIO
& GREGORY WOLFE

SL/.NT
BOOKS

LIVING THE LITURGY
A Witness

Slant Books
P.O. Box 60295
Seattle, WA 98160

www.slantbooks.org

Cataloguing-in-Publication data:

Names: Giussani, Luigi.

Title: Living the liturgy: a witness / Luigi Giussani.

Description: Seattle, WA: Slant Books, 2024

Identifiers: ISBN 978-1-63982-160-0 (hardcover) | ISBN 978-1-63982-159-4 (paperback) | ISBN 978-1-63982-161-7 (ebook)

Subjects: LCSH: Giussani, Luigi | Catholic Church—Liturgy | Catholic Church—Liturgy—Calendar | Catholic Church—Liturgy—Theology

CONTENTS

INTRODUCTION

Francesco Braschi

"IN ITS WIDEST SENSE, the liturgy is humanity made aware
that the adoration of God is its supreme meaning, and that work
is the glory of God." We should begin from a similar breadth of
horizon if we want to approach this text of Father Giussani, which
we can define as both *synthetic* and *fundamental*, with a genuine
awareness of its meaning and value.

The *synthetic* character of the book comes not only from the
circumstances of its origin (as the Note to the First Edition re-
lates, it consists of "quick notes" collected from conversations that
took place over eight years, from 1965 to 1973) but above all in its
original intention. In these pages, in fact, Father Giussani strives
to offer a comprehensive perspective and to teach a method that is
capable of introducing us to the Christian liturgy as it is lived by
the people of God. At the same time—and this is not to be taken
for granted—he respects all the fullness and depth of meaning
that the liturgy holds: for the vocation of each believer and, above
all, by its nature as *Opus Dei*, the objective evidence of the presence
of God as the subject of history.

For this reason, the meditations that we have in our hands
reveal right away a characteristic that makes them stand out in
the panorama of contemporary texts that flourished after the

liturgical reform of the Second Vatican Council; that is, they avoid two approaches—only apparently opposed to each other—those of *archeology* and *liturgical sociology*.

The first approach consists not only in the literary-historical analysis of texts, of ritual forms and their development (an approach which is licit and indispensable for a correct comprehension of the Church's patrimony), but also in the clarification of the conditions for the correct celebration (through research of the most ancient texts) as *the* fundamental problem of the liturgy, to be resolved first by singling out the historical period taken as a paradigm (often accompanied by a devaluation of other moments in liturgical history) with its reconstruction in the mentality and contemporary praxis of individuals and communities.

Liturgical sociology, on the other hand, does not pay particular attention to the historical aspect but concentrates on researching the communication techniques that are held to be necessary for the rite to be adequate to the necessities and the receptive capacities of contemporary man (which often are limited and strongly concentrated on the horizontal-community dimension of the ritual gestures). If these techniques are not respected—they say—it would be difficult or even impossible to comprehend the liturgical action; this action would be in some way condemned to practical inefficacy.

Both of these positions—interchangeable in many different ways, as recent history shows—have in common a double risk: on one side, they see the liturgy as an activity the success of which resides first of all in the capacity of those (scholars, teachers, celebrants) who have the task of guiding it; on the other hand, they assign to themselves the limited task of "representing" (in the form that they hold to be correct) a reality—the relationship with God—that is substantiated and built elsewhere and that is in some way "made appropriate" to the individual believer and the community.

SUCH WAYS OF UNDERSTANDING the liturgy are not purely theoretical or able to be relegated to the years of the conciliar and post-conciliar reform but rather represent a true challenge for the faith as Pope Benedict XVI authoritatively reminded us at the Heiligenkreuz monastery in 2007 when, while speaking to the Cistercian monks, he said: "In all our efforts on behalf of the liturgy, the determining factor must always be our looking to God. We stand before God—he speaks to us and we speak to him. Whenever in our thinking we are only concerned about making the liturgy attractive, interesting and beautiful, the battle is already lost. Either it is *Opus Dei*, with God as its specific subject, or it is not." And, on the same occasion, he added a parallel link between liturgy and theology: "In its desire to be recognized as a rigorously scientific discipline in the modern sense, theology can lose the life-breath given by faith. But just as a liturgy which no longer looks to God is already in its death throes, so too a theology which no longer draws its life-breath from faith ceases to be theology; it ends up as an array of more or less loosely connected disciplines" (Benedict XVI, Address at Heiligenkreuz Abbey, Austria, 9 September 2007).

From a distance of over ten years, in a context that sees the crumbling of the values most necessary to life, the meaning of these words is not only relevant but even more urgent, because the liturgy—even to those who still profess themselves to be believing and practicing Christians—often appears as a container to be filled with activities (or better, activism) or a place to live on the wave of sentiment, grabbing a few phrases or expressions that strike us at the moment.

We cannot escape from the clarity with which Pope Benedict specified that *the forgetfulness of the theological character of the liturgy and its intrinsic link with faith* is the ultimate reason for the frequent polarization (when it is not an outright contradiction) that is often seen, for example, between celebration and life, between liturgical archaism and instances of renewal, between faithfulness to tradition and creativity in celebration, between the modality of the approach to the word of God which they sharply separate—as if they were two different objects—the personal meditation of the Bible and its liturgical proclamation, between the horizontal-communitarian and vertical-theological . . . until you end up with a deconstruction that fragments the Christian experience, reducing it to a series of irresolvable dualisms.

The Pope emeritus calls us to refuse every reductive approach, to look at the liturgy recognizing first of all that God is its *present subject* and that the essence of every celebratory action is the possibility of a gaze toward Him—because it is always from Him that the dialogue with humanity moves. This constitutes therefore an important indication of method, to be grasped before every other pastoral consideration, because it is useful to find again *the nexus between liturgy and faith*: a vital and constitutive link for both terms.

This is precisely the method of Father Giussani in these meditations. And this clarity of formulation makes the meditations that are re-proposed here—after 50 years—surprisingly current.

Their *synthetic* character, which we have already noted, can now be explained in the will and the capacity of the author to locate himself at a level that puts itself *before* any partiality: Father Giussani himself underlines it in the *Preface*:

> If it is true that we can be struck in front of a phrase or some other text of the liturgy, we should be attentive not to reduce the richness of this meditation to a selection of phrases. This is not the center of the problem. We must educate ourselves not to meditate in that way on the liturgy because we would commit an error. Or, more than an error, a diminishing, a reduction of the attitude and the value of the presence of God. This reduction has happened often: the Bible, which is the story of the mystery of God in the world, was treated as the source of beautiful, just, and profound phrases, but this leaves to the side the context, the true word of God. In this way, we reduce the Bible to a support for our moral ideals. Instead of understanding the discourse of God as the new language that shatters our human wisdom, we have taken the word of God as a support for our wisdom, or even treated the Bible in an accommodating sense—that is, when a passage is interpreted according to the ear of our cultural mentality, instead of searching to make that

mentality adequate to the meaning, to the communication, to the witness that sprang from this phrase.

We should approach the individual phrases of the
liturgy as highlighted instances of a unique word. We
should not spell them out, but harmonize them with the
life of Christ in the Church. The liturgy is a conversation
that does not end and is carried along by the power of
grace, by the mystery of God in the world.

The correct way to approach the liturgy (to "harmonize" and not
to "spell out," that is, to break up the syllables, like a child who is
learning to read) is to place ourselves as consciously as possible
in front of a discourse that is *other* than our discourses, and to
welcome "the discourse of God as the new language that shatters
our human wisdom." Consequently, every attempt to assimilate
the Christian liturgy to a naturally human rituality, or to reduce it
to a purely cultural or sociological discourse, not only constitutes a
grave error of method (by not understanding the object, the word
of God and His Presence in the world) but even more deeply, reveals the radical misrepresentation of the person who is the second
actor (because the principal actor, as we have seen, is the Mystery),
not as a participant or spectator of a sectarian cultural fact, but
starting from the radicality of his nature as one "called," the object
of a vocation.

And so Giussani affirms in the first lines of this book: "belonging to the mystery of the Church," in fact, constitutes "the
ultimate and complete determinant of our vocation"; but precisely
this "liturgical event" is revealed to be that "typical moment of
the life of the Church" meditating on which constitutes an "act of
adequate vigilance on the path that each of us has been assigned."
We are thus led by the hand to grasp what is the *fundamental* character of this book: the gaze on the liturgy that it fosters is an act
that consolidates the vocational path of every believer (the path
of life called to a faith that is recognized as vocation), anchoring
it directly in the action of God which is *objectively recognizable*,
present in the grace of the Sacraments.

Another keyword for understanding these pages is the reference to a *lived* liturgy. In Giussani's mind, this term is not exhausted in the eminently *practical* character of the reflections, stripped of every academicism and proposed to those who already participate daily in the liturgy. The *lived* liturgy is, for the author, the movement that is produced by the encounter between the Christian rite and the vocation of the individual, which we have first described as the true *method* for this encounter to become a living experience. This experience has a precise form, according to Giussani. In fact, "The lived liturgy constitutes the path of our morality" (p. XVIII) because its words enunciate the way that leads to conversion of heart, the newness that clothes "perception and judgment, feeling, decision, and action" (p. XIX) when listened to with obedience.

But this obedient listening, Giussani adds, beyond fostering conversion, defines our life understood as the expectation of the coming of the Lord, a coming that from the "place" of the liturgy passes then to daily life, which is vivified and nourished with meaning in the movement of the liturgical seasons, in which we are helped to "incarnate" the practice of the Sacraments (especially Confession and the Eucharist), connecting this practice to the presence of Christ in the world and in time.

THIS SUMMARY PRESENTATION OF the fundamental points of the Preface, following the method suggested by Giussani, which is the essential starting point to immerse ourselves in the more detailed meditations that constitute the rest of the text, already helps us intuit the richness of the perspective that is offered.

The *first part* of the volume takes up and describes the radicality of Giussani's approach to the sacrifice of the Mass: that gesture which—he affirms—is for us "the most important gesture in the whole history of the world," that is, "the death and resurrection of Christ." Even in this case, the nexus with the concrete experience of each believer is quickly established. Every believer is called to recognize in the Mass, and in every single gesture that constitutes it, "the paradigm, the intelligence, the inspiration, the impetus, the

force of correcting everything, the capacity to understand everything, so that everything has meaning" (p. 2). The description of
the different moments of the ritual never indulges in erudition
as an end in itself: on the contrary, there is a constant call at the
fundamental level to a judgment of faith, to the recognition that
"the judgment of the value on my life and on that of the world
is Christ dead and risen" (p. 6), which fact is never relegated to a
group of past events, but which even today "is investing history . . .
according to the presence that is moving the world to its destiny
through our lives" (emphasis ours).

The *second part*, dedicated to the liturgical seasons and to a
few of the most important feasts in the year (Advent, Christmas,
Lent, Easter, Ascension, Pentecost, Trinity), is characterized by
the detailed treatment of the modalities of the presence of Christ
in history. But this word "history," already so dense in meaning, receives in Giussani's reading a plurality of senses: the liturgical year,
in fact, in its articulation from Advent to Easter, represents the
totality of the events of the Covenant between God and human
beings (from the expectation of Israel to the coming of Christ,
to the fulfillment of Easter and the time of the Church) but also
the history of the personal encounter of each believer with the
Mystery in the appropriation of the human event of the Savior
and the generation of man and of the new people for whom Easter
becomes the criterion of authenticity of the whole of individual
and communitarian existence.

Thus, Advent is "the time of expectation, the time of the first
sign of unity between our freedom and the freedom of God" (p.
23), which was lived by the prophets and now is proposed to us
as the passage from *our* images and expectations of God to the
welcoming of His being as Mystery. Christmas is the entrance
into the world of "a new reality, a new presence," starting from
which "certainty becomes objective" with an interest only in the
capacity that this newness of life possesses to "overwhelm each of
us" (p. 32). Lent signals the time of "conversion," understood first
of all as the moment in which "the Word, the Christian discourse,
should be born from our personal gaze on Jesus Christ," and the

Lenten liturgy "is the supreme affirmation of this salvation that has come, Jesus Christ" (p. 41). Easter is "the definitive . . . which has already happened," that "the world must journey again to comprehend" and whose hope "calls us out and makes us different from our environment" (p. 64). Ascension is the moment in which our Christian vocation becomes authentic—paradoxically—in the absence of the "manifestations of the power of Christ according to the mode of our expectation," because in those conditions "his action coincides, is identified with the motivations and the working of our person" (p. 72). Pentecost manifests how the Holy Spirit may be in us "the principle of knowledge of the Father and the Son" as an "event existentially fulfilled" (p. 79).

The liturgy of the Most Holy Trinity, chosen by Father Giussani as the volume's point of arrival, is "the foundational meditation, the alpha and omega of everything," a "mystery hidden even though it has been revealed . . . which we will not be able to exhaust even in eternity when we will see Him face to face" and is defined as "the mystery of security, the mystery of certainty" (pp. 88, 89).

To let ourselves be guided by Father Giussani on this itinerary means being helped continually to recognize the richness and the coherence of the Christian path, of *every* Christian path: the path of the individual, of the community who celebrates, of the vocational companionship, of the entire Church, of creation as the work of God, directed toward Him as its fulfillment. The loss of horizon that continually afflicts and impoverishes our existence, marked as it is by individualism—often visible in the realm of prayer and liturgy—is a constant reminder of the absence of the person and finds in this volume an antidote, a medicine, that consists in the continual reconstruction of that openness of reason which the lived liturgy promotes, as little by little the presence of the Mystery is objectively revealed and attested.

And so, the *testimony* that emanates from the lived liturgy is also—in the first place—the testimony of Father Giussani himself, in his capacity of incarnating this comprehensive and totalizing gaze on reality, which to his eyes was truly the transparency of the presence of Christ. This gaze becomes available to us as well through these pages, whose nature demands that they not be read "sitting down" but rather as a kind of *vademecum*, to have in hand as we walk and as we look around us, to be able to continually enjoy an intelligence of reality that we continue to face. We remain grateful for an experience that is still possible and that is witness to the vitality of the charism entrusted to Father Giussani.

PREFACE

THE FACT THAT GATHERS all of us together as the People of God is our belonging to the mystery of the Church.

The Church is the source of our personality, the ultimate and fullest determinant of our vocation. Therefore, in order to bring about an awareness that is appropriate to the path that each of us has been assigned, our meditation must do nothing other than follow the essential moment of the Church's life: that of the liturgical event.

In its widest sense, the liturgy is humanity made aware that the adoration of God is its supreme meaning, and that work is the glory of God. The beginning of the liturgical year, therefore, should always be the beginning or the renewal of an awareness that gives our life its true shape, that manifests in us the new creature willed by God, according to obedience to the Father. Each of us must respond to God and to the call of the mystery of the Church according to the grace that has been given to us, according to the "talent" that has been entrusted to us.

Saint Paul says: *Dum tempus habemus, operemur bonum* (Galatians 6:10). While we have time, let us act in accordance with the good. *Tempus* indicates the hour and the content of the hour; it corresponds therefore to the term "occasion." And this occasion is the word that has been spoken to us, the possibility that has been offered, an energy that we feel and that cannot be offered to us the hour after.

This meditation on the liturgy is a meditation on the educational discourse given by the Church. Therefore, it is ever more valuable the more we grasp the word that the Church wants to say to us at a particular moment in the year. If it is true that we can be struck in front of a phrase or some other text of the liturgy, we should be attentive not to reduce the richness of this meditation to a selection of phrases. This is not the center of the problem. We must educate ourselves not to meditate in that way on the liturgy because we would commit an error. Or, more than an error, a diminishing—a reduction—of the attitude and the value of the presence of God. This reduction has happened often: the Bible, which is the story of the mystery of God in the world, was treated as the source of beautiful, just, and profound phrases, but this leaves to the side the context, the true word of God. In this way, we reduce the Bible to a support for our moral ideals. Instead of understanding the discourse of God as the new language that shatters our human wisdom, we have taken the word of God as a support for our wisdom, or even treated the Bible in an accommodating sense, that is, when a phrase is not interpreted according to our ear—to the ear of our mentality, of our culture—instead of searching to make our mentality, our culture, adequate to the meaning, to the communication, to the witness that sprang from this phrase.

We must approach individual phrases of the liturgy as resonances (words and phrases that resonate in different ways) of a unique word. We must not look at the words in isolation but harmonize them with the life of Christ in the Church. The liturgy is an unending conversation and it is carried along by the power of grace, by the mystery of God in the world.

The lived liturgy constitutes, very simply, the path of our morality. By morality, we mean the right attitude, the right behavior, "right" in front of destiny, the right attitude on the path of destiny.

The liturgy is the synthetic and simple enunciation of this path.

In fact, Christian morality is nothing other than the conversion of our heart, the turning of our heart in the exact direction, the direction which indicates the new "heart": a new perception and judgment, feeling, decision, and action.

This morality, understood as conversion, is defined by two great categories.

The first is the category of listening. The liturgy is a book for the poor of spirit, for those who do not invent their own words. The faithful Christian people follow, repeat, and respond to the liturgical word. Therefore, the liturgy is the place of obedience. There is no path of conversion that does not include this obedience of the heart.

The liturgy is first of all listening, and, because it is first of all listening, it is the word that initiates conversion. *Lex Domini irreprehensibilis convertens animas* (Psalm 18:8). The word of the Lord is irreproachable; it is precise and changes the soul. The word of the Lord in history is the liturgy.

Because the beginning of conversion is listening, the liturgy is the place where we await the coming of the Lord. In fact, when a person prays or reads, eats or works, what is he really doing, if he is a Christian, if his heart has been converted? He is just awaiting the coming of the Lord. In the measure the Christian lives this awaiting, he changes everything that he has in his hands. And so, the Lord's coming has already begun for him.

The first factor of Christian morality, therefore, is listening and awaiting the Lord's coming, which is in its depth the attitude of the poor in spirit. If one has nothing else, one listens. If one has nothing else, one waits, and so one hopes to become different.

The second factor of Christian morality is the totality of commitment to the grace of the mystery of God. We live our whole life within this "grace" that reaches us with the liturgical life of the Church and its sacraments.

On the one hand, in fact, the liturgy has the sacraments as its center: the final words of the conversation, the events in which the divine action is realized, the presence of the community as mystery; and on the other hand, the particular liturgy clarifies the meaning of the sacraments: Confession and Eucharist in the Christmas season, for example, have a particular significance different from those sacraments in the Easter season. In each moment, though, all the shades of meaning are present together.

Now, if we do not include everything in this grace, we divide Christ and the world, almost as if we made Christ a presence in the world over whom we had rights.

Instead, the conversion of the heart which happens to the poor of spirit generates the unity of the person. Outside of this, whatever energy we think we have, whatever personality we feel ourselves to possess, we will be divided. Divided: Christ/world, community/world, person and activity in the world.

This conversion of heart, the event of those who are poor in spirit, which generates unity in the person, has only one channel: the liturgy. One riverbed into which, in the measure it is lived, all the water of our life is poured: eating and drinking, speaking and praying, working. And so, wherever we are, the dawn of the new world, His coming, begins to break.

PART I

The Mass

THE MOST IMPORTANT GESTURE in the entire history of the world is the death and resurrection of Christ. In our life, this gesture is the sacrifice of the Mass. It should be at the center of our day, its most important, privileged moment. It should have an influence on our day. (We must remember that, in order for a gesture to influence life, it should cost something; to cost means work, engagement of our energies, and attention. A gesture that does not cost something is not true.)

The Mass is, then, the most important gesture of our existence because it is the gesture of the death and resurrection of Christ. If in fact we say that we are part of the body of Christ, members of each other, the Mass is the supreme expression of the Christian assembly, of that permanent assembly which is the Christian life. The Mass is the supreme gesture of the community, of the hidden mystery of Christ and of His Church: "Truly you are a God who hides himself, O God of Israel, the Savior!" (Isaiah 45:15).[1]

Faith is a new judgment on reality, on "what makes life worth living." Everything derives from the response we give to this question. One such response is referred to in the Scripture when it says: "The just one will live by faith" (Habakkuk 2:4). Faith is a judgment about the value of life and of the world that has its source in the gesture of Christ's death and resurrection, which we remember. In this gesture, communion with Him, with the Father and with the Spirit, is revived, is reborn continually.

All this is expressed in the Mass with real force. And in fact, all of the Christian life should be a lived Mass; the Mass should be the paradigm, the ideal, inspirational structure, the form of all our actions. We are called to bring to life the mystery of the Christian assembly in which we remember the death and resurrection of Christ. All our gestures, therefore, excluding none, are implied in the Mass. Saint Paul expresses it well when he says: "So whether you eat or drink, or whatever you do, do everything for the glory of God" (1 Corinthians 10:31); or in this beautiful passage from the Letter to the Romans: "None of us lives for oneself, and no one dies for oneself. For if we live, we live for the Lord, and if we die, we die for the Lord; so then, whether we live or die, we are the Lord's" (14:7-8).

All of our gestures, however small, have the structure of the mystery of the death and resurrection of Christ, that is, the structure of the Mass.

All of our gestures should find in the mystery of the Christian assembly, in which we remember the death and resurrection of Christ, the paradigm, the intelligence, the inspiration, the impetus, the correction of everything, the capacity to understand everything, because everything has a meaning.

So, even just briefly, we must formulate the consequences of the Mass for our personal life.

A great American philosopher of the last century, Alfred North Whitehead, said: "Religion is what the individual does with his own solitariness."[2] We must remember, though, that word religion has the Latin root of binding and indicates a phenomenon that binds together, that connects all of reality, because it binds us to God and to everything. The "I" is linked to God, a relationship with God. So God is everything, not just as a way of speaking, but because it is true. It is true.

God is everything "of you," "in you."

For this reason, the topics that we will touch on summarily are meant to be an invitation to participate in the Mass as a contribution to our personal conversion.

There is no other scheme for this change in our personality than that of the sacramental gesture.

The Mass is a unifying gesture, but it is constituted by different parts that bring to life the various factors of a unique reality.

By following intelligently the parts of the Mass, we will be able to comprehend the characteristics of every action of our lives—which should be the characteristics of every relationship, of every day, of every project.

In the name of the Father, and of the Son, and of the Holy Spirit

THE MASS STARTS IN this way. And soon after we say: "The grace of our Lord Jesus Christ, and the love of God and the communion of the Holy Spirit be with you all." Or that which is the same: "The Lord be with you."

This is the premise of faith, a judgment on life by which we recognize that the meaning of my existence, of your existence, of everybody's existence, of the whole history of the world, is named Jesus Christ. It is the mystery of the Trinity, the mystery of God who is one and three, of God who is communion. It is the mystery of this God who revealed Himself by coming among us.

The Bible says at a certain point: before you pray, prepare your conscience so that you don't seem like a man who tempts God.[3]

The introductory phrases of the Mass recall the consciousness of what we are, of the value of the flesh, the bones, and the spirit of each, the value of woman and of man, of friendship, of errors, of difficulties and evil. They recall the substance of everything.

> In the beginning was the Word, and the Word was with God, and the Word was God. He was in the beginning with God. All things came to be through him, and without him nothing came to be. What came to be through him was life, and this life was the light of the human race; the light shines in the darkness, and the darkness has not overcome it. A man named John was sent from God. He came for testimony, to testify to the light, so that all might believe through him. He was not the light, but came to testify to the light.
>
> The true light, which enlightens everyone, was coming into the world. He was in the world, and the world came to be through him, but the world did not know him. He came to what was his own, but his own people did not accept him. But to those who did accept him he gave power to become children of God, to those who believe in his name, who were born not by natural generation nor by human choice nor by a man's decision but of God. And the Word became flesh and made his

dwelling among us, and we saw his glory, the glory as of the Father's only Son, full of grace and truth.

John testified to him and cried out, saying, "This was he of whom I said, 'The one who is coming after me ranks ahead of me because he existed before me.'" From his fullness we have all received, grace in place of grace, because while the law was given through Moses, grace and truth came through Jesus Christ. No one has ever seen God. The only Son, God, who is at the Father's side, has revealed him. (John 1:1-18)

I say this so that no one may deceive you by specious arguments. For even if I am absent in the flesh, yet I am with you in spirit, rejoicing as I observe your good order and the firmness of your faith in Christ. So, as you received Christ Jesus the Lord, walk in him, rooted in him and built upon him and established in the faith as you were taught, abounding in thanksgiving. See to it that no one captivate you with an empty, seductive philosophy according to human tradition, according to the elemental powers of the world and not according to Christ. For in him dwells the whole fullness of the deity bodily, and you share in this fullness in him, who is the head of every Principality and Power. In him you were also circumcised with a circumcision not administered by hand, by stripping off the carnal body, with the circumcision of Christ. You were buried with him in baptism, in which you were also raised with him through faith in the power of God, who raised him from the dead.

And even when you were dead [in] transgressions and the uncircumcision of your flesh, he brought you to life along with him, having forgiven us all our transgressions; obliterating the bond against us, with its legal claims, which was opposed to us, he also removed it from our midst, nailing it to the cross; despoiling the principalities and the powers, he made a public spectacle of them, leading them away in triumph by it. Let no one, then, pass judgment on you in matters of food and drink or with regard to a festival or new moon or sabbath. These are shadows of things to come; the reality belongs to Christ.

Let no one disqualify you, delighting in self-abasement and worship of angels, taking his stand on visions, inflated without reason by his fleshly mind, and not holding closely to the head, from whom the whole body, supported and held together by its ligaments and bonds, achieves the growth that comes from God. If you died with Christ to the elemental powers of the world, why do you submit to regulations as if you were still living in the world? "Do not handle! Do not taste! Do not touch!" These are all things destined to perish with use; they accord with human precepts and teachings. While they have a semblance of wisdom in rigor of devotion and self-abasement and severity to the body, they are of no value against gratification of the flesh. (Colossians 2:4-23)

The awareness of all this should be the premise of all our actions, of all our decisions, great or small.

The passage from Saint John that was cited announces that Christ is the substance of everything. If we stop believing it, it does not cease to be true. In Him everything has consistence. This is our faith, this is the faith of the Church that we glory in professing.[4]

This must become like a "habit," or better a *habitus*—that is, a permanent attitude—which in philosophical terms is called virtue. Virtue, in fact, is a permanent form of the correct energy. In a converted life, virtue is the awareness of the presence of Christ, the memory of Christ who is present. This awareness of the presence of Christ in everything and in everyone is the content of our vigilance, which means that this awareness accompanies us in every action. It is true change. Love, friendship, work, everything is a sad lie if in these things we do not take note of the mystery of the reign of the God who has knocked at our door. In that case, change does not happen, the conversion of mentality. "He came to what was his own, but his own people did not accept him" (John 1:11).

In the Name of the Father

IN HEBREW, "NAME" INDICATED the power of a person. Therefore, "in the name of" means to recognize that all things are sustained by the power of God, that everything is God.

Here, the premise of every action is vigilance: we call it continual prayer. To live vigilantly is to live with intelligence, to live with our full personality.

But do we see this continual prayer in ourselves? Do we have a facility with this type of vision, with this memory, this gaze on the death and resurrection of Christ, of that historic Christ who is present even if we don't think of him? The *habitus*—habituating ourselves to this, the *desire* to habituate ourselves to this—makes it more easily achievable.

The judgment of value on my life and on the world is Christ dead and risen. He did not live two thousand years ago and that's it. Everything that's happened since is investing history, not according to fleshly forms—as Saint Paul says (2 Corinthians 5)—but according to a presence that is moving the world to its destiny through our existences. "It was not you who chose me, but I who chose you" (John 15:16).

Brothers and sisters, let us acknowledge our sins, and so prepare ourselves to celebrate the sacred mysteries.

THE FIRST FUNDAMENTAL FACTOR of a converted action, of a Christian action, is the awareness of our own sin. No authentic moment of our existence can avoid this self-accusation, with the exception of Our Lady. She had the awareness of a transparency, the awareness of the fact that everything had been given to her. "My soul magnifies the Lord because he has done great things for me" (Luke 1:46-48).

But for us this "magnifying the Lord" means first of all recognizing that God makes us walk, makes us part of His Church, despite the fact that we are liars. Sin, in fact, is a lie: the affirmation that the meaning of life, what makes life worth living, is something other than Christ.

Hear, O heavens, and listen, O earth, for the Lord speaks: Sons have I raised and reared, but they have rebelled against me! An ox knows its owner, and an ass, its master's manger, but Israel does not know, my people has not understood.

Ah! Sinful nation, people laden with wickedness, evil offspring, corrupt children!

They have forsaken the Lord, spurned the Holy One of Israel, apostatized. Why would you yet be struck, that you continue to rebel? The whole head is sick, the whole heart faint. From the sole of the foot to the head there is no sound spot in it, just bruise and welt and oozing wound, not drained, or bandaged, or eased with salve.

Your country is waste, your cities burnt with fire; your land—before your eyes strangers devour it, a waste, like the devastation of Sodom and Gomorrah.

And daughter Zion is left like a hut in a vineyard, like a shed in a melon patch, like a city blockaded.

If the Lord of hosts had not left us a small remnant, we would have become as Sodom, would have resembled Gomorrah.

Hear the word of the Lord, princes of Sodom! Listen to the instruction of our God, people of Gomorrah!

What do I care for the multitude of your sacrifices? says the Lord. I have had enough of whole-burnt rams and fat of fatlings; in the blood of calves, lambs, and goats I find no pleasure.

When you come to appear before me, who asks these things of you? Trample my courts no more! To bring offerings is useless; incense is an abomination to me. New moon and sabbath, calling assemblies—festive convocations with wickedness—these I cannot bear. Your new moons and festivals I detest; they weigh me down, I tire of the load. When you spread out your hands, I will close my eyes to you; though you pray the more, I will not listen. Your hands are full of blood!

Wash yourselves clean! Put away your misdeeds from before my eyes; cease doing evil; learn to do good. Make justice your aim: redress the wronged, hear the orphan's plea, defend the widow. Come now, let us set things right, says the Lord: Though your sins be like scarlet, they may become white as snow; though they be red like crimson, they may become white as wool. If you are willing, and obey, you shall eat the good things of the land; but if you refuse and resist, you shall be eaten by the sword: for the mouth of the Lord has spoken! (Isaiah 1:2-20)

Thus says the Lord through Isaiah, and these observations of the Bible are categories that have value for our life.

There is nothing healthier than the realistic awareness of the condition in which we must carry out an action. There is no healthier gesture, at the origin of every action, than the awareness that we are sinners. At least, at the minimum, we should recognize that even our simplest actions lack the awareness of vigilance, the intensity of faith. We render poor things that should be full of richness.

And we usually sin in two ways; these are the roots of our disproportion.

First, *the reluctance to commit our lives: saying "no" to faith.*

Now someone approached him and said, "Teacher, what good must I do to gain eternal life?" He answered him, "Why do you ask me about the good? There is only One who is good. If you wish to enter into life, keep the commandments." He asked him, "Which ones?" And Jesus replied, *"You shall not kill; you shall not commit adultery; you shall not steal; you shall not bear false witness; honor your father and your mother'; and 'you shall love your neighbor as yourself."* The young man said to him, "All of these I have observed. What do I still lack?" Jesus said to him, "If you wish to be perfect, go, sell what you have and give to the poor, and you will have treasure in heaven. Then come, follow me." When the young man heard this statement, he went away sad, for he had many possessions. Then Jesus said to his disciples, "Amen, I say to you, it will be hard for one who is rich to enter the kingdom of heaven. Again I say to you, it is easier for a camel to pass through the eye of a needle than for one who is rich to enter the kingdom of God." (Matthew 19:16-24)

Even if we have faith, we flee from faith, because faith is a commitment that mobilizes us, that transforms us, that pushes us to change.

The second source of our sins is that *we do not hope for the solution of our individual and collective problems from faithfulness to Christ*, and therefore we do not expect joy from Him. We see it also in the history of the people of Israel, which God gave as a paradigm of the life of the people of God, of our life.

> Therefore, thus says the Holy One of Israel: Because you reject this word, and put your trust in oppression and deceit, and depend on them, this iniquity of yours shall be like a descending rift bulging out in a high wall whose crash comes suddenly, in an instant, crashing like a potter's jar smashed beyond rescue, and among its fragments cannot be found a sherd to scoop fire from the hearth or dip water from the cistern. For thus says the Lord God, the Holy One of Israel: "By waiting and by calm you shall be saved, in quiet and in trust shall be your strength." But this you did not will. "No," you said, "Upon horses we will flee." Very well, you shall flee! "Upon swift steeds we will ride." Very well, swift shall be your pursuers! A thousand shall tremble at the threat of one—if five threaten, you shall flee. You will then be left like a flagstaff on a mountaintop, like a flag on a hill. (Isaiah 30:12-17)

> Woe to [those who] go down to Egypt for help, who rely on horses; who put their trust in chariots because of their number, and in horsemen because of their combined power, but look not to the Holy One of Israel nor seek the Lord! Yet he too is wise and will bring disaster; he will not turn from his threats. He will rise up against the house of the wicked and against those who help evildoers. The Egyptians are human beings, not God, their horses flesh, not spirit. (Isaiah 31:1-3)

In these passages from the Bible, chosen as examples, God asks His people not to put their faith in anyone but Him. Have we not said that faith is a judgment of value on the world? And the judgment is that Christ is everything in everyone and without Him nothing can be done. All things have their consistence in Him: the rocks, the stars, and man, society, the past and the future. "This is our faith, the faith of the Church which we glory in professing" (Rite of Baptism).

So then, the second root of every sin of ours: even we trust ourselves to "Egypt"—the biblical symbol of the enemy of God—and not to the Lord, the true God.

The Word of God

THE WORD OF GOD helps us understand the disproportion between us and the ideal of Christ but also connects us to this ideal.

In fact, in the Mass, after the gesture of contrition, we pass to the proclamation of the word of God with the passage from the Old Testament, the Epistle, the Gospel.

We do not understand the passages we read during the Mass if listening to these words does not produce in us the awareness that we are sinners. Only through this real contrition is it possible to participate in the gesture of the community that is happening in that moment. In this way, we can hear the deep call of the word of God—the call of faith.

We should realize that too frequently this call, these words, are heard with a great detachment.

But what does it mean to live the faith? To live the faith is not something different from living life. It means to live life with the instinct, the intelligence, the heart, and the will of faith.

We can no longer say to ourselves: "Okay. We are Christians: but in the problems of life and of society what should we do?" This kind of question highlights how our personality has been broken in two, almost as if the judgment about life, about society, about culture were outside of the horizon of faith. Nothing is outside the confines of the experience of faith because its boundaries are the boundaries of life. "The just one will live by faith" (Habakkuk 2:4; Hebrews 10:38), says the Lord.

A faith that has the fact of Christ as its content, that is, the event of the one in whom all things consist, is characterized by this integrity—well beyond integralism—for which all of life is handed over to God, by which we adhere to an announcement that says: nothing of you is yours.

To live the faith means that it informs everything, as a conception, as a feeling, as a project, as a decision, as a way of facing things. Saint Paul says, when he writes to the Philippians: "Whatever is true, whatever is honorable, whatever is just, whatever is pure, whatever is lovely, whatever is gracious, if there is any excellence and if there is anything worthy of praise, think about these things" (4:8). There are not good things and bad things for us Christians; there is, rather, a way of facing things with faith or without faith. This is how good and evil are established, the evil that wears out, destroys, and corrupts reality. We are very good at casting blame when instead we should understand that our infidelity creates hardship and corruption. If then the word of God illumines our life, accompanying it with the awareness of our disproportion, the pain we always see in our actions is a healthy pain, is constructive, is a pain that does not block us, that pushes us to be better—what Saint Paul calls "godly sadness" (2 Corinthians 7:9-10). "Evil sadness," instead, is the pain that interrupts the construction, the melancholy that becomes lament. "Godly sadness" has the same point of departure, notes the disproportion, but does not stop there: it generates a pain that turns us around, that converts us. The awareness of our sin changes us, fills us with the desire to change our life.

The word of God converts life, changes the meaning of life, always, every day. This inexhaustible vitality which the word of God raises up in us is the truth that remains for eternity.

Offertory

THE OFFERTORY IS THE gesture to which the word of God pushes us.

"Blessed are you Lord God of all creation. Through your goodness we have this bread to offer, fruit of the earth and work of human hands, it will become for us the bread of life." And also for the wine.

The bread and the wine are the signs which indicate everything that is important in our life: the relationship with our families, our studies, our work, whatever we truly value. This "bread" and this "wine," this fruit of the situation, of our freedom and of our work, indicate the whole of life.

What then does the prayer of offertory mean?

It means that, illuminated by the word of God, we desire our whole life to be created for faith. Therefore we symbolically offer to God ourselves, our body, our spirit, everything that will happen in our day, our life, everything. This "bread" and this "wine" are us; they are the offering of ourselves.

After having pronounced the formulas of offering, the priest bows before the altar and says, in a barely-audible voice, this beautiful invocation: "With humble spirit and contrite heart may we be accepted by you, O Lord, and may our sacrifice in your sight this day be pleasing to you, Lord God."[5]

Without humility, the whole gesture is immediately corrupted by a lie. In fact, how can we make this gesture of offering? Who would be capable of translating everything into the terms of faith? All we can do in life is cry out to God to take what is His to Himself. The offertory is this cry.

The priest at the offertory takes the chalice, puts in a drop of water and says: "By the mystery of this water and wine may we come to share in the divinity of Christ who humbled Himself to share in our humanity."[6]

Christ has assumed our human nature. Only by staying united to Christ can things be transformed, transfigured.

But, how do we stay united to Christ? Saint John says, in the seventeenth chapter of his Gospel: "so that they may all be one, as you, Father, are in me and I in you, that they also may be in us, that the world may believe that you sent me" (17:21).

The reality of Christ is the reality of the mystery of the Church. And the Church is not simply "all of us put together"; it implies, of course, all of us, but it is also something much greater, because it is the mystery of Christ. So the true problem is to live the life of the Church.

We will change in the measure we live the life of the Church. How does a child become an adult, with an adult mentality, capable of facing life, with a sensibility that invests everything with a moral structure? The child learns this mentality, builds this sensibility, creates this moral structure by being involved with the life of his parents. The more the family is truly an environment for the child, the more the child will grow with a solid personality, without dissociations, without distortions.

What did Christ say in order to change people? "Come with me" (Matthew 19:21; John 1:39).

How terrible is the illusion of being able to do things on our own, as if man were not a plant that gains strength only if it is planted in the right soil. And the soil of human personality is the community. For us Christians, it is the Christian community, the Church.

The offertory of the Mass is the culminating moment, in which we enter into the play of God, with our freedom.

We say to God: all life is Yours, therefore I cry out to You, take my life. Because our life is not changed by ourselves: the mystery of Christ who works in us changes our life.

The condition that makes it possible to carry out the gesture of the offertory is to have the awareness that we are part of the mystery of Christ, the Church.

Consecration

AFTER THE OFFERTORY COMES the consecration, the supreme moment of the Mass. Right after the *Sanctus*, the priest extends his hands over the bread and wine saying: "You are holy, Father, the fount of all holiness. . . ."[7] Holy and holiness are words that indicate the truth of things, adding to the idea of truth the concept that something is true only if it is as God wills, because it is God who creates everything. The words holiness, or true personality, realization of life, perfection, total satisfaction, or happiness, are similar words.

When the priest says, "Make holy, therefore, these gifts, we pray, by sending down your spirit upon them like the dewfall," it means that he is asking God to make true, authentic, the relationships with friends, with one's wife, with one's husband, with colleagues. To make them true, that is, full of faith, because truth lives only in faith.

And when the priest continues, saying: "So that they may become for us the body and blood of Christ," he is not reciting an empty formula, because Christ has really penetrated history as a mystical body, the body of which everyone is a member. Saint Paul says: "For all of you who were baptized into Christ have clothed yourselves with Christ. There is neither Jew nor Greek, there is neither slave nor free person, there is not male and female; for you are all one in Christ Jesus" (Galatians 3:27-28). This is the new creature who has entered into the world, and therefore all of our actions are called to become expressions of the reality of Christ in the world.

And in fact, the prayer at the center of the Consecration says: "At the time he was betrayed and entered willingly into his Passion, he took bread and, giving thanks, broke it, and gave it to his disciples, saying: 'Take this, all of you, and eat of it, for this is my body, which will be given up for you.'" The words are repeated for the chalice and then conclude saying: "Do this in memory of me." Everything in us cries out to God in the prayer that is at the center of the Mass: everything should become the body and blood of

Christ, part of the mystery of Christ that has already liberated the world with His death and resurrection, but that invests our actions with the possibility of collaborating in this liberation. The whole world is in need of our faith, of our life that is changed by faith, of our life that has become the death and resurrection of Christ at work in history.

> See, days are coming—oracle of the Lord—when I will make a new covenant with the house of Israel and the house of Judah. It will not be like the covenant I made with their ancestors the day I took them by the hand to lead them out of the land of Egypt. They broke my covenant, though I was their master—oracle of the Lord. But this is the covenant I will make with the house of Israel after those days—oracle of the Lord. I will place my law within them, and write it upon their hearts; I will be their God, and they shall be my people. They will no longer teach their friends and relatives, "Know the Lord!" Everyone, from least to greatest, shall know me—oracle of the Lord—for I will forgive their iniquity and no longer remember their sin. (Jeremiah 31:31-34)

But what does it mean for all of our actions to become the gesture of Christ? It means that they should be lived in faith, that is, in union with Christ, the union that is realized in the life of the Church.

The Church is the mystery of Christ in the world, the fruit of the irreversible covenant which in the Mass is offered in the sacrifice of the body and blood of Christ: "The new and eternal covenant."[8] The Covenant of the Old Testament means that God involved Himself in the history of the people of Israel, but for us today that is only a symbol of the final involvement that God assumed when He became one of us and died and rose for us. Christ is God who came to liberate us. And therefore the goal for which life exists is already among us, is like a seed under the earth, is Christ risen. That which the world will be at the end, the true love of man and woman, the true and eternal friendship, has entered into history and is also within us, in the deepest structure of our being through Baptism. All nations, though, must be brought within this Covenant, through faith in the death and resurrection of Christ.

Our Father

AT THE END OF the Consecration, the Church has us recite the Our Father, with which the central part of the Mass is concluded. We are called in this way to remember that all our actions are part of a great design which is the design of the Father. And so Jesus, when He teaches us how to pray, helps us to remember, if we repeat His words, that our actions have only one aim: that His kingdom come. Every gesture lived without this awareness of being part of the design of God is blurred, out of focus—for the one doing the gesture is more or less alienated. "Our Father, your kingdom come, your will be done" (Matthew 6:9-13; Luke 11:2-4). Without this awareness, the gesture would be lost—for its truth for human history, for the liberation of the world, for the good of men.

The fulness of His truth is recovered only in the awareness of those who live in faith. In that awareness lies the "consecration" of life. These words "consecrated" or "holy" might bring to mind something partial or limited; they are, rather, words that indicate a global fact, because the consecration of life to God signifies the truth of love, of work, of research, of justice, of life itself. All of life is transfigured. From this conversion of life, the true change of the world begins even now. Every other point of departure is presumptuous and false. We are dealing here with that wisdom of God which, as Saint Paul says in his letter to the Corinthians, is foolishness to the world (1 Corinthians 1:23).

Everything that we do must enter into the design of God.

This conviction, this awareness, and the will to carry it forward, are the fulcrum of the whole Christian moral life.

Our conversion will happen in proportion to our capacity to base our lives truly on this fulcrum, even if we remain sinners. We will understand, we will feel, we will do things fundamentally differently while remaining sinners. God, in fact, even consecrates our evil through the greatest sign of His power: forgiveness. We are called to live even our evil according to faith, which means accepting the forgiveness of God. Thus, not even our evil will be able to stop us.

For this reason, the Our Father, after saying "Your kingdom come," concludes with these words: "But deliver us from evil." Liberation from evil means living in such a way that our sin does not become a prison, a cause of blockage: or better, that sin does not end up as a program, even though it remains a continually painful possibility of incoherence, through our weakness and wickedness. This liberation permits a continual recovery of the path, an invincibility in not letting ourselves be beaten down by our errors; liberation comes from the awareness that God is stronger than our weakness or wickedness.

Grant peace to our days

THE WORD PEACE GOVERNS the whole liturgy before Communion. The prayer that comes right after the Our Father says: "*Grant peace in our days*, that, by the help of your mercy, we may be always free from sin and safe from all distress, as we await the blessed hope and the coming of our Savior, Jesus Christ."[9] This is a magnificent analysis of peace as the visible consequence of faith. Peace means that sin will never stop us, and this is possible only with the help of the mercy of God, and only in this way are we free from all distress, from all anxiety, because we are supported by the only solid ground. Expectation, then, defines the clarity of the horizon and of the end, without which peace cannot be complete.

The Bible defines God as "my mercy" (Psalm 58:18). God for man is mercy, and the peace that lives within us has only one name: the mercy of God. We can only build on the foundation of peace; in war we get distorted and are destroyed.

The most comprehensive and definitive word of what God is for man is forgiveness: I forgive you, God says to the people of Israel; you always do evil, you always rebel, but I forgive you because I am God and not man (Hosea 11:9). For man, true forgiveness is impossible because this word means to be born again.

The relationship with God, instead, renews: "Though your sins be like scarlet, they may become white as snow; though they be red like crimson, they may become white as wool" (Isaiah 1:18).

Our worldly reality is linked to, conditioned by, what we do. Instead, man is free because God frees him. Our past life becomes new and everything cooperates for the good, even our evil. It is terrible how we Christians can go weeks, years, without feeling that deep abandonment to the mercy of the one who has loved us and given Himself for us.

"I live, no longer I, but Christ lives in me; insofar as I now live in the flesh, I live by faith in the Son of God who has loved me and given himself up for me" (Galatians 2:20). If God is with me, who can condemn me? This is what Saint Paul says in the Letter to the Romans (8:31). We do not have this sense of peace because we do not have a sense of true contrition. Peace is determined by our capacity for contrition. Every time, in fact, that God speaks to man, he begins His discourse in this way: do not let your hearts be troubled, do not be afraid (John 14:1,27). This is not an irresponsible pietism, but rather a lived responsibility.

In the following prayer of the liturgy, the priest says from the altar: "The peace of the Lord be with you always. Let us offer each other the sign of peace." This means that he invites us to have *peace among ourselves*. The peace that exists between people who socially might be strangers is certainly another miracle—it challenges the world because it is impossible outside of a Christian mentality.

I will underline a few factors of this fraternal peace.

It does not murmur

IT IS NOT POSSIBLE, first of all, to be embraced by the mercy of God made flesh, which is communion, and to gossip about a brother or sister. This is the work of Satan: to spread evil. I speak of gossip because calumny is also a blasphemy against the truth, an expansion of evil in the world. The one who gossips has a taste for evil. When I recognize a brother or a sister who has a defect and who has failed, all the while remaining mindful of my own defects, I will find a horror at my own sins when I look at the fault of the other.

It is not wrathful

SAINT PAUL SAYS: "Do not get angry with each other," but also adds: "Do not let the sun go down on your wrath" (Ephesians 4:26). Wrath is a kind of madness in us.

Not to be wrathful is to be patient. Patience is like the figure of Atlas, the man who carries the world on his shoulders. "By your perseverance you will secure your lives" (Luke 21:19). Patience is the contrary of wrath, which demands that things change quickly or be different.

It does not close the heart

FINALLY, WE ASK OURSELVES: How is it possible to recognize a need among us that does not have repercussions for everyone? Through the realization of this real, practical fraternity, our individualism changes. Only Christ destroys the individualistic way of conceiving man and things. It takes time, but through this fraternity the world is challenged with the miracle that it cannot perform: unity among men and women. "Let us offer each other the sign of peace."[10] It is a symbol of an embrace that is much bigger, much more profound and real. The process of realizing this unity is the flip side of the process of knowledge: we gain knowledge when we gather together, when we understand that the Church that calls us is Christ who calls everyone, but these true things always begin to come about in small ways.

This peace with ourselves, among ourselves, becomes objective in structures of life, in living together, and in this way, our passion, our intelligence, our energy in the interests of the world is empowered. Our peace is not a fleeing into the desert; our fraternity, our unity does not make a fortress from which we never exit. It generates a passion for the world, for work and its problems, for social life, a passion for the world according to the temperament, the vocation, and the situation of each person.

Gathering together to celebrate the Mass does not resolve problems in a technical way. But celebrating the Mass teaches us the exact position from which to face the problems of work. We know what we cannot give up; we know the encompassing idea on the basis of which we can carry out all our activities.

The Mass reveals what kind of subject we are. It sets the actor in the great drama of the world.

Communion

AND SO, THE LITURGY of the Mass prepares us to carry out in a conscious way the gesture of sacramental communion.

The meaning of what the Church says in that beautiful invocation, soon after the *Sanctus*, becomes clear: "Humbly we pray that, partaking of the Body and Blood of Christ, we may be gathered into one by the Holy Spirit."[11]

This is the ideal happiness of the world: to give unity to the world. And through our communion with the body and blood of Christ, through the communion of our actions with Christ, through the consecration of our life, the Spirit will bring about the union of men and women in one body. This is our faith: the faith which carves out in the superficial, carnal face of things, the awareness of that mysterious action of the Spirit. For this reason, we say that the first contribution of Christians to the political, social, human liberation of the world is to live the faith—that is, to live communion—understood as the singular gesture of the Mass, but also as a factor and dimension of life.

PART II

Liturgical Times and Feast Days

Chapter 1

ADVENT

THE TIME OF ADVENT IS the time of expectation, the time of that first hint of union between our freedom and God's. It is the time of the Old Testament, of what must be fulfilled, of the path.

In the prophets, expectation, the expectation of the Messiah—inspired by God and accepted by them—was formulated according to the ideas, the sensations, and the mentalities that belonged to them, as a race and as individuals, in that moment. Their expectation, inevitably, was formulated according to their feelings, their concepts, and their aspirations. They were a people in the desert, and God was for them "the earth which flourishes"; they were slaves, and they thought that the kingdom of God was power, their predominance in the world; they were divided, and for them, the kingdom of God was the unity of the people.

They identified the mystery of God with their concept and thus forgot that God is mystery. While their conception led them toward the mystery, their inability to let go of their own ideas became an obstacle to the kingdom of God.

Today, the Church continually recalls us to this sense of mystery.

There is no season of the liturgical year that does not remind us that God is mystery. This call to mystery becomes expectation. We are expectation: our life is expectation. We know that this expectation is a mystery in its origin because that is how we have been made, and mystery is also its ultimate destination.

Even for us, expectation translates itself into our ideas, conceptions, fears, in our image of good and evil, virtue and sin. Expectation is incarnated in all these things. All of life is a prophecy of God for us, that is, of the kingdom of God.

But this kingdom is always different, unforeseeable, because what is of God is always unforeseeable. Therefore, woe to those who place an insurmountable obstacle between the event of sin and God; woe to those who refuse forgiveness. This is the crisis of expectation: the danger that our thoughts, our feelings, will block us, will rot in us. While everything is a good and cooperates for the good, nothing exhausts the mystery, yet everything is a prophecy of the mystery, the point from which an unforeseeable development begins.

Deep down, our error in understanding the law of expectation happens when we wait for the kingdom of God without truly wanting "that" kingdom, wanting the kingdom to happen without truly loving the kingdom of God. The Pharisees, for example, truly wanted the kingdom of God to come—they loved the law—but they were unable to love what would happen. We can do everything for the kingdom of God, without loving its modalities with conviction and truth. This is the residue of a moralism in us, the last bit that never gives in, that does not love what happens. We do not allow our own "I" to dissolve, to disappear, to lose itself in His name. So, one can do many great activities yet lack charity. But precisely when one recognizes that he has failed in this way, God purifies him down to the marrow of his bones: in the discovery of our resistance, we understand what love is, who God is for us.

We need to remember that God is faithful: he has raised up this expectation in order to fulfill it. Every type of justice will be satisfied.

> Asked by the Pharisees when the kingdom of God would come, he said in reply, "The coming of the kingdom of God cannot be observed and no one will announce, 'Look, here it is,' or, 'There it is.' For behold, the kingdom of God is among you."

Then he said to his disciples, "The days will come when you will long to see one of the days of the Son of Man, but you will not see it. There will be those who will say to you, 'Look, there he is,' or 'Look, here he is.' Do not go off, do not run in pursuit. For just as lightning flashes and lights up the sky from one side to the other, so will the Son of Man be in his day. But first he must suffer greatly and be rejected by this generation. As it was in the days of Noah, so it will be in the days of the Son of Man; they were eating and drinking, marrying and giving in marriage up to the day that Noah entered the ark, and the flood came and destroyed them all. Similarly, as it was in the days of Lot: they were eating, drinking, buying, selling, planting, building; on the day when Lot left Sodom, fire and brimstone rained from the sky to destroy them all. So it will be on the day the Son of Man is revealed. "On that day, a person who is on the housetop and whose belongings are in the house must not go down to get them, and likewise a person in the field must not return to what was left behind. Remember the wife of Lot. Whoever seeks to preserve his life will lose it, but whoever loses it will save it. I tell you, on that night there will be two people in one bed; one will be taken, the other left. And there will be two women grinding meal together; one will be taken, the other left. There will be two men in the field; one will be taken, the other left behind." (Luke 17:20-36)

Our meditation on expectation will focus on a few fundamental factors.

Our life will be judged, because nothing is saved except through judgment. Saint Paul compares this judgment to a fire that burns up everything but the truth: if things are gold or silver, if they are wood or chaff, this will appear through fire—through judgment. Out of this judgment, the design of God will appear, as we see in the passage of the Gospel above, and therefore, the truth of things will appear once again. Through this judgment, our recognition of the design of God will appear and, consequently, the truth with which we do things. The truth with which we look at things will appear as well as the truth with which we handle things, because—as the Gospel says—then everything will be clear. It will be clear in the sense that the light will come; as Jesus pointed out, "There is nothing hidden that will not become visible, and nothing secret that will not be known and come to light" (Luke 8:17).

> "Immediately after the tribulation of those days *the sun will be darkened, and the moon will not give its light, and the stars will fall from the sky, and the powers of the heavens will be shaken.* And then the sign of the Son of Man will appear in heaven, and all the tribes of the earth will mourn, and *they will see the Son of Man coming upon the clouds of heaven* with power and great glory. And he will send out his angels with a trumpet blast, and they will gather his elect from the four winds, from one end of the heavens to the other." (Matthew 24:29-31)

> "But of that day and hour no one knows, neither the angels of heaven, nor the Son, but the Father alone. For as it was in the days of Noah, so it will be at the coming of the Son of Man. In those days before the flood, they were eating and drinking, marrying and giving in marriage, up to the day that Noah entered the ark. They did not know until the flood came and carried them all away. So will it be also at the coming of the Son of Man. Two men will be out in the field; one will be taken, and one will be left. Two women will be grinding at the mill; one will be taken, and one will be left. Therefore, stay awake! For you do not know on which day your Lord will come." (Matthew 24:36-42)

We must underline another thing in addition to this impending judgment: *the sense of the precariousness of life*, "for the world in its present form is passing away" (1 Corinthians 7:31).

> "Beware that your hearts do not become drowsy from carousing and drunkenness and the anxieties of daily life, and that day catch you by surprise like a trap. For that day will assault everyone who lives on the face of the earth. Be vigilant at all times and pray that you have the strength to escape the tribulations that are imminent and to stand before the Son of Man." (Luke 21:34-36)

"Gird your loins and light your lamps and be like servants who await their master's return from a wedding, ready to open immediately when he comes and knocks. Blessed are those servants whom the master finds vigilant on his arrival. Amen, I say to you, he will gird himself, have them recline at table, and proceed to wait on them. And should he come in the second or third watch and find them prepared in this way, blessed are those servants. Be sure of this: if the master of the house had known the hour when the thief was coming, he would not have let his house be broken into. You also must be prepared, for at an hour you do not expect, the Son of Man will come." (Luke 12:35-40)

But, paradoxically, in the things that happen there is a call to a responsibility that we cannot avoid, just like we cannot hide from the gaze of God (Psalm 139). The final judgment is in fact made actual, literally, in the trials of life. These trials anticipate the final judgment: trials of whatever nature, physical or moral, but above all the trials that put our faithfulness to God in crisis. These are the test of our trust; they may be an objection for us, but not for God.

The final judgment, after all, is the culmination of those judgments that happen through the trials that God gives us. The trial makes us understand that the final moment brings to light all the other moments of our life.

THE LITURGY OF ADVENT, at the beginning of the new year, rightly recalls the end of the road itself, the conclusion of the road and the goal of time. The conclusion of the road and the goal of time happen when Christ returns and when things will be, truly and finally, what they should be.

Everything will be truly itself because the light of God will not be impeded anymore by anything and Christ will have fulfilled His work, so that everything will truly belong to Christ, as Christ belongs to God (1 Corinthians 3:23). We cannot approach the sanctuary of God if not through a judgment, a judgment of value on existence and on history, a judgment that tests the strength of our time and our history. All our sins, our uncertainties, our reluctance, and all our running away are born from the absence, from the weakness, of judgment in us. And it is the word of God that forms the basis for this judgment in us. As the word of God will establish the judgment at the end of life, so also the word of God establishes the judgment on what happens to us now: in the word of God, every crisis is conquered, the trial is overcome, we are freed from evil.

> "When the Son of Man comes in his glory, and all the angels with him, he will sit upon his glorious throne, and all the nations will be assembled before him. And he will separate them one from another, as a shepherd separates the sheep from the goats. He will place the sheep on his right and the goats on his left. Then the king will say to those on his right, 'Come, you who are blessed by my Father. Inherit the kingdom prepared for you from the foundation of the world. For I was hungry and you gave me food, I was thirsty and you gave me drink, a stranger and you welcomed me, naked and you clothed me, ill and you cared for me, in prison and you visited me.' Then the righteous will answer him and say, 'Lord, when did we see you hungry and feed you, or thirsty and give you drink? When did we see you a stranger and welcome you, or naked and clothe you? When did we see you ill or in prison, and visit you?' And the king will say to them in reply, 'Amen, I say to you, whatever you did for one of these least brothers of mine, you did for me.'
>
> "Then he will say to those on his left, 'Depart from me, you accursed, into the eternal fire prepared for the devil and his angels. For I was hungry and you gave me no food, I was thirsty and you gave me no drink, a stranger and you gave me no welcome, naked and you gave me no clothing, ill and in prison, and you did not care for me.' Then they will answer and say, 'Lord, when did we see you hungry or thirsty or a stranger or naked or ill or in prison, and not minister to your needs?' He will answer them, 'Amen, I say to you, what you did not do for one of these least ones, you did not do for me.' And these will go off to eternal punishment, but the righteous to eternal life." (Matthew 25:31-46)

Love is patient, love is kind. It is not jealous, love is not pompous, it is not inflated, it is not rude, it does not seek its own interests, it is not quick-tempered, it does not brood over injury, it does not rejoice over wrongdoing but rejoices with the truth. It bears all things, believes all things, hopes all things, endures all things. Love never fails. (1 Corinthians 13:4-8)

These passages from Saint Matthew and Saint Paul, in a summary yet definitive way, describe the criterion of the final judgment, but also the criterion of the judgments that happen in the trials of life. The trial crushes the one who does not live in the dimensions of love. Saint John of the Cross says: "At the end of our life, we shall be judged on our love."[12] Love is not a discourse, but rather placing your own life within the Discourse (the Word). In the name of this Discourse, our way of life changes, a change that can only be true if we change at the root. Otherwise, we do nothing other than accentuate the mask that we already wear, and when a mask is worn in the name of the Holy Spirit, it is infinitely worse.

We do not have any other program but the program of charity, and charity is not a feeling or a particular inclination to do well, or a compassion, or a commiseration, or a wave of affection, but the actualization of the judgment that has happened in us.

In Advent, the only theme is "He who comes" and the visible and sensible signs of "He who comes" are the new relationships that exist between us.

The conversion brought by Christ is a concrete fact; the love of God for men is a reality in the womb of a woman—a fetus, a baby who is born, a man, therefore a tangible, sensible, physical reality. The recognition of this fact among us translates, at the same time, into a physical, experienceable, sensible, new reality.

The awareness of the imminence of His coming, therefore, the vigilance—a life lived in the awareness of ourselves as expectation—makes new relationships emerge.

And this happens in proportion to the memory of Christ that we live, in proportion to the prayer that we are, in proportion to the silence that we have at the depth of all our actions.

His coming is His judgment; therefore, our actions should transform themselves into charity, into communion.

But in order for our actions to become judgment and anticipate His coming, in order for the Church to be built and for our work to become the house of God and the place for the oppressed, the blind, the stranger, the widow, the orphan, we need *patience*.

"Be patient, therefore, brothers, until the coming of the Lord. See how the farmer waits for the precious fruit of the earth, being patient with it until it receives the early and the late rains. You too must be patient. Make your hearts firm, because the coming of the Lord is at hand" (James 5:7-8). His coming is imminent even if we have to walk for two thousand years.

"Take as an example of hardship and patience, brothers, the prophets who spoke in the name of the Lord" (James 5:10).

And when our patience, which is so poor, is about to give way, like Ahaz in the book of Isaiah, then the Lord will come: "Again the Lord spoke to Ahaz: 'Ask for a sign from the Lord, your God; let it be deep as the netherworld, or high as the sky!' But Ahaz answered, 'I will not ask! I will not tempt the Lord!' Then he said: 'Listen, house of David! Is it not enough that you weary human beings? Must you also weary my God? Therefore the Lord himself will give you a sign; the virgin shall conceive and bear a son, and shall name him Emmanuel'" (Isaiah 7:10-14).

At the extreme end of our patience, His sign will appear among us.

So the story of Israel went ahead without an apparent logic, always with something new, and often with something that seemed to contradict the initial direction, whether it be idols or exile or corruption—into which Emmanuel, God with us, came. Therefore, the freedom of God goes beyond what we could imagine.

The imminence of His coming, and the charity that anticipates the final judgment, means that we build new relationships. And this building relies on our personal responsibility and initiative: that others recognize these relationships is the task of God. "My hour has not yet come," Jesus said to Our Lady at the wedding of Cana.

Patience and dignity render us free in every action and, at the same time, present in everything.

Chapter 2

CHRISTMAS

WITH THE NATIVITY, A NEW reality, a new presence, has entered the world. Certainty becomes objective. The presence of the Word is not just an appearance that could deceive us.

The announcement of this newness of life, of this presence, interests us in so far as it extends its impact to each one of us. The aim of the Incarnation is to assimilate us to His divinity. The Word was made flesh . . . to assume us into Himself.

This overcoming of the banal and the ephemeral, this divine in the human, aims essentially to identify us with Him, to bring us within His measure.

After the Nativity, ours is a new presence.

LET US UNDERLINE, first of all, the factor that is at the root of this mystery. This factor is at the origin of our Christian commitment and determines everything: it is *the Father*. It is, in fact, mercy, the power of the Father, that generates the Nativity; Christ among us manifests His benevolence, His charity. The Father is the mover of everything. For this reason, the first authority at the origins of our Christian life—there is no other—is the will of the Father alone.

Religiosity lies in this: in doing "what is pleasing to the Father" (John 8:29). We can, in fact, have a passion for Jesus Christ and not be religious if we lack this sense of mystery. Our adoration of the Father is the guarantee of the truth even of our love for

Christ because it is the mystery that is not reducible to sentimentality or dialectic—it is mystery-authority.

Let us try now to look at these affirmations in their methodological and moral application.

Let us ask ourselves: what does Christ's phrase, "I always do what is pleasing to the Father," mean? It is the indication of a way of acting that has, as its fundamental dimension, *obedience*.

Now the original authority, the source of everything, becomes clear to us through an event. The announcement, the message, is an event. If, therefore, the authoritative source is made clear in the event, it becomes—as a consequence—an authority in our life.

In the Bible, the missionary dialogue between the Father and the Son, from which is born the redemption of the world, is imagined as a dialogue of obedience: "Here I am! Send me!" (Isaiah 6:8). The mystery of the Incarnation, of Christmas, is the mystery of obedience. And so, the death and resurrection of Christ are the obedience to the definitive power of the Father. And this definitive power is Christ: He is the obedient one.

> "My Father is at work until now, so I am at work" (John 5:17).
>
> "Amen, amen, I say to you, a son cannot do anything on his own, but only what he sees his father doing" (John 5:19).
>
> "I cannot do anything on my own; I judge as I hear, and my judgment is just, because I do not seek my own will but the will of the one who sent me" (John 5:30).
>
> "I came down from heaven not to do my own will but the will of the one who sent me" (John 6:38).
>
> "My teaching is not my own but is from the one who sent me" (John 7:16).
>
> "I know Him, because I am from Him, and He sent me" (John 7:29).
>
> "I do nothing on my own, but I say only what the Father taught me" (John 8:28).

"I tell you what I have seen in the Father's presence"
(John 8:38).

Obedience to the Father that gives consistency to this new
subject who will preach, who will die on the cross, who will rise
from the dead and create the Church, is obedience to the *design*
of the Father, understandable only in concrete, historical, ordinary
terms, made up of encounters, events, things.

The supreme call of the Mystery of Christmas is the establishment of obedience in the world. In this way, humanity grasps the
profound peace that comes from finding the right position: that
of the creature. "Peace on earth to those who await His coming."

We can only build from a foundation of peace.

The Lord, who came to rebuild, to remake man, the world (a
man, if he is not born again, cannot see the kingdom of God [John
3:3]), came bringing peace as His first gift.

"Hail Mary, full of grace, the Lord is with you" (Luke 1:28).
This is the peace, the security of the design of God over us: in the
word that God has spoken and speaks to us, in His design that
involves us.

This security in the God who calls us, in His order, is faith.

"My just one shall live by faith" (Habakkuk 2:4; Hebrews
10:38).

The grace of Christmas is the grace of peace, which is the
fruit of faith, of security in His word.

At the end of Advent, of expectation (certain that He will
come), there is another certainty: the certainty that God has already come, that He is already at work in us.

Peace, the feeling that our life is founded on a certitude, is
sustained with God's power; it has its origin in our awareness of
the authority of the Father.

The more there is, in us, the awareness of our relationship to
the Father, the more everything is stable in our life. Analogously,
in the fascinating gratuity, in the beauty that is full of that event
in which we perceive and discover the meaning of everything in
His memory (in the strong sense: "Do this in *memory* of me"),
here lies the true tranquility of our work. If we are not grounded

in this supreme security, we have to keep giving ourselves things to do from morning to evening to feel calm, to justify ourselves. We need to be faithful to that Fact, that is, to be aware of it—and awareness of it is awareness of self.

In His agony, Jesus Christ brought three people along with Him and was sad because they could not stay awake with Him. It is the same for us. That peace that is born from relationship with the Father, the security by which we are supported by another, by something that comes before us, is made evident in the communion with those who are engaged in the same event.

The "memory" of this generates a companionship for the whole of life. This companionship is not an alternative to anything, because it is a dimension of our "I," a place of inspiration, not of competence or organization in our action.

The deeper the sense of the Father, the more powerful and ineradicable is the communion with those whom God has put close to us (Christ sacrifices Himself above all for those whom God has put close to Him). It is a communion that is like the permanence of the event, the objectivization of the relationship with meaning, a communion that lies behind all I do, like the motor of my actions (for this reason it is not an alternative to anything, it leaves nothing out).

This sense of the Father is the heart of the charity which determines my attitude toward everything else. If we do not cling to this original and originating charity, we will have less charity toward others because it will be either more foolish (not comprehending its motivation) or more individualistic (born ultimately from our choice).

Peace lives as hope.

The people of God, our communion, is the place of this hope.

Peace is the certainty in "the appearance of the glory of our savior Jesus Christ" (Titus 2:13).

The manifestation of Our Lord Jesus Christ follows the design of the Father, and the law which indicates this following is the word *incarnation*: *a faith within the world*.

The Father, revealing Himself to us, has given us the Son within a precise, structured reality: he was born on *that* night in *that* situation, he was known by *that* people, he was circumcised like the other Hebrews, he was given a name that had been assigned Him.

Therefore, the moment of the world in which we are living is the modality of the incarnation. Christ totally adheres to these modalities: "He had to become like his brothers in every way" (Hebrews 2:17).

The terms of the situation in which God puts us are so clear, the modality in which this faith is incarnated is so concrete, that the particular climate, the needs of the world and of our society, all point to the form that our testimony and the presence of our faith must take.

A faith within the world: our time is such that this "within" becomes an inevitable part of the design that God has for us. To be means that one must be within. To pull away from the world would certainly be an exceptional vocation in this historical moment. It is only hope—the hope given by faith—that makes one incarnate that faith within the world.

It would seem that we are concrete to the extent that we act, and maybe we are disappointed in ourselves when we do not act. It would seem that our work is what gives consistency to our faith, but this is a terrible error.

If it is not born from faith and hope, the incarnation becomes a sort of refuge, an impatience with the cross, a claim to a certain type of support. It is "not jumping" and "having one foot in two shoes." The incarnation is born of faith, lives in hope, is *charity*: otherwise, it is worth nothing and would not give peace.

An incarnate faith that truly sacrifices itself is charity, is the announcement of a new reality, is "the day the Lord has made" (Psalm 118:24).

Faith, hope, charity are the principles by which the supernatural, which is within us invisibly, makes itself experienceable, the principles of a new identification with God, of a new birth in us, of a mysterious unity with Christ.

WE CAN GRASP THE nature of our true work in the attitude of the shepherds: "When they saw this, they made known the message that had been told them about this child" (Luke 2:17).

"Then the shepherds returned, *glorifying and praising* God for all they had heard and seen, just as it had been told to them" (Luke 2:20).

Christ is communicated to us through the mission of others; and we make known, like the shepherds, what He has communicated to us: this manifestation is the same gesture as praising and glorifying God.

The joy of Christmas is born and expressed as the possession of something—the announcement—that is not ours, but is from another: a joy that is pure love, pure altruism. This is why Christmas is the feast of the child—in the evangelical sense—that is, of simplicity.

Insofar as we are able to rejoice in someone other than ourselves, we complete the circle of God the creator and God the redeemer, because this simplicity is nothing other than the appearance of what we are deep down: expectation of an other. If there were not in us at least a grain of this simplicity, we would not be able to welcome God, nor acknowledge that the announcement is true, that it corresponds to us and to our expectation.

The liturgy of the Nativity is also the liturgy of Our Lady: "Blessed are you who believed that what was spoken to you by the Lord would be fulfilled" (Luke 1:45).

Blessed, that is, for no other reason than being entrusted with the announcement.

Blessedness, the truth of the Christian life, depends only on the purity with which we accept and live the announcement, the purity that was in Mary, in the shepherds, in the magi.

"During those days Mary set out and traveled to the hill country *in haste*" (Luke 1:39).

"In haste" corresponds to what Saint Paul said in chapter 9 of the Second Letter to the Corinthians: "God loves a cheerful giver" (2 Corinthians 9:7).

> Mary set out and traveled to the hill country in haste to a town of Judah, where she entered the house of Zechariah and greeted Elizabeth. When Elizabeth heard Mary's greeting, the infant leaped in her womb, and Elizabeth, filled with the holy Spirit, cried out in a loud voice and said, "Most blessed are you among women, and blessed is the fruit of your womb. And how does this happen to me, that the mother of my Lord should come to me? For at the moment the sound of your greeting reached my ears, the infant in my womb leaped for joy. Blessed are you who believed that what was spoken to you by the Lord would be fulfilled." (Luke 1:39-45)

Let us think about what that event meant for Our Lady and how she was obedient to it.

There is an analogy to be made with our existence, in which God "calls" us through privileged moments.

What I am referring to is an event that can, of course, be repeated at various times in our life but that has a precise beginning that can be seen. There are, in fact, moments that make themselves clear with a fundamental authority, and all the others—each with its own irremovable and permanent function—are the development and the deepening of that original event.

It is the type of event that is eminently revelatory, illuminating all the rest, like the experience of Pentecost for the Apostles. Pentecost did not eliminate the moments of Calvary and the Resurrection but illuminated, explained, made them significant. In this—in this event of "light"—the authority of the Father is revealed and the history of our relationship with the Church acquires a strength of meaning and therefore places itself at the root of our personality: it begins a new word, a new discourse in our life. Thus, as the authority reveals itself as "idea-norm," this event represents the original moment in our Christian life, not from the ontological point of view (which is Baptism) but from the point of view of authority (the event which makes us understand the meaning of our Baptism).

Our function, the contribution of our person, of our specific richness, the communion in which our personality reposes and is nourished, to which our "I" refers itself with the same fullness with which it is grasped, the communion which gives inspiration—all of this is shaped by this revelatory event, all of this gives meaning to our Christian existence.

The specificity of this encounter and the communion it creates is not an alternative to anything but makes possible, reasonable, full of sympathy, our communion with everything, our dedication to the world. This specificity and communion are constitutive of our "I," part of our character and not external factors.

As we move, act, live with our particular character, we move and live with this clarifying inspiration and this inspiring communion that comes from the announcement we have received. It is a type of event that throws light also on the most constitutive facts of our personal existence; therefore, we always do what "pleases" that fact. We always move on the wave of that announcement; all our action communicates—is missionary—from that announcement.

Otherwise, what would it mean to dedicate ourselves to others? It would be a series of reactions without meaning, an activity whose criterion would be rooted, ultimately, in the reaction of our "I." Whereas the Father does everything with a design, makes each thing a function of the whole.

If one pole—in the dialectic that the mystery of the Nativity represents for us—is the figure of Mary, the other is the witness of the saints; if the first term is the welcoming of the announcement, the other is a testimony to that announcement.

The feasts of the saints that follow immediately after Christmas proclaim this idea of testimony at the coming of the Lord into the world and find their meaning in the Epiphany: the manifestation of the Lord to the whole world, because His coming is for the whole world.

We spend our whole life giving witness to Him, communicating to everyone that He has come. The Christian, in fact, is not better than others; he is simply the one who has received the task of communicating the announcement, the joy of Christmas, to others. Therefore, the task of the Christian, as such, is not that of revolutionizing structures but of communicating the announcement—an announcement that cannot be communicated, though, unless we become companions to men and women. From this comes the engagement with everything human—and so also with structures—which is a consequence and a vehicle, because the value of all man's engagement comes from the transcendent ("Without me you can do nothing" [John 15:5]; "Martha, Martha, you are anxious and worried about many things. There is need of only one thing" [Luke 10:41]). The awareness of the disproportion that exists between our doing and the eschatological, transcendent point has its origin here. Our task is that of announcing, "The Lord has come, therefore take comfort and do not be afraid." Our passion for giving witness makes us, as Saint Paul said, everything to everyone (1 Corinthians 9:22).

In the Christmas season, the Word that has been communicated to us—the Word that remakes the world, that builds it—continues to call us.

We need to desire Christ as the "Everything" of our own life and the life of the world.

This is possible in faith, and faith is a judgment that recognizes the value and the implications of the Fact that has happened among men.

Chapter 3

LENT

THERE COMES A TIME WHEN the Word, the Christian discourse, must be born from our own personal looking at Jesus Christ. It is, in fact, Jesus Christ the Word who is at the center of our Lenten meditation.

If the theme of Advent was that of a global expectation, if the time of Christmas was the announcement of the salvation that has come and begun to manifest itself, the liturgy of Lent is *the supreme affirmation of this salvation that has occurred* in Jesus Christ—Jesus Christ who is Lord of man, of nature, of the cosmos, of the world, and of its whole history; Jesus Christ in the precise contours of His maturity, in the clear definition of His mission, in His face that is unmistakable, present among all human things. The mature figure of Christ, the new man, is made clear through the power of His newness. A new measure has entered the world, a new proposal has entered life, a measure and a proposal that are so new that the whole of life is played out in accepting this new measure or in sinking under as slaves of the old.

But the measure of the mystery of God is a mature person, a formed personality, who moves as a presence that we cannot flee, through our friendships, our houses, our work environments and interests, who personally confronts each of us. The entirety of faith is here: all of faith is in the face we take on, in the gaze we bring to this Person, in the reaction that we have to His presence.

The Lenten liturgy illuminates this presence, the magnificence of His proposal, the concreteness of His figure in the Gospels. The Samaritan woman: this man who sees into the depths from whom no one can flee, whom no one can avoid; for whom we truly need to go to the depths, never halfway. The Gospel about Abraham[13]—"If you remain in my word, you will truly be my disciples" (John 8:31)—anything less than this would be a lie. The Gospel of the man born blind who is healed and of Lazarus raised from the dead: the power with which He governs things and time.

> He had to pass through Samaria. So he came to a town of Samaria called Sychar, near the plot of land that Jacob had given to his son Joseph. Jacob's well was there. Jesus, tired from his journey, sat down there at the well. It was about noon.
>
> A woman of Samaria came to draw water. Jesus said to her, "Give me a drink." His disciples had gone into the town to buy food. The Samaritan woman said to him, "How can you, a Jew, ask me, a Samaritan woman, for a drink?" (For Jews use nothing in common with Samaritans.)
>
> Jesus answered and said to her, "If you knew the gift of God and who is saying to you, 'Give me a drink,' you would have asked him and he would have given you living water." The woman said to him, "Sir, you do not even have a bucket and the well is deep; where then can you get this living water? Are you greater than our father Jacob, who gave us this well and drank from it himself with his children and his flocks?" Jesus answered and said to her, "Everyone who drinks this water will be thirsty again; but whoever drinks the water I shall give will never thirst; the water I shall give will become in him a spring of water welling up to eternal life."
>
> The woman said to him, "Sir, give me this water, so that I may not be thirsty or have to keep coming here to draw water." Jesus said to her, "Go call your husband and come back." The woman answered and said to him, "I do not have a husband." Jesus answered her, "You are right in saying, 'I do not have a husband.' For you have had five husbands, and the one you have now is not your

husband. What you have said is true." The woman said to him, "Sir, I can see that you are a prophet. Our ancestors worshiped on this mountain; but you people say that the place to worship is in Jerusalem." Jesus said to her, "Believe me, woman, the hour is coming when you will worship the Father neither on this mountain nor in Jerusalem. You people worship what you do not understand; we worship what we understand, because salvation is from the Jews. But the hour is coming, and is now here, when true worshipers will worship the Father in Spirit and truth; and indeed the Father seeks such people to worship him. God is Spirit, and those who worship him must worship in Spirit and truth."

The woman said to him, "I know that the Messiah is coming, the one called the Anointed; when he comes, he will tell us everything." Jesus said to her, "I am he, the one who is speaking with you."

At that moment his disciples returned, and were amazed that he was talking with a woman, but still no one said, "What are you looking for?" or "Why are you talking with her?"

The woman left her water jar and went into the town and said to the people, "Come see a man who told me everything I have done. Could he possibly be the Messiah?"

They went out of the town and came to him.

Meanwhile, the disciples urged him, "Rabbi, eat." But he said to them, "I have food to eat of which you do not know." So the disciples said to one another, "Could someone have brought him something to eat?" Jesus said to them, "My food is to do the will of the one who sent me and to finish his work. Do you not say, 'In four months the harvest will be here'? I tell you, look up and see the fields ripe for the harvest. The reaper is already receiving his payment and gathering crops for eternal life, so that the sower and reaper can rejoice together. For here the saying is verified that 'One sows and another reaps.' I sent you to reap what you have not worked for; others have done the work, and you are sharing the fruits of their work."

Many of the Samaritans of that town began to believe in him because of the word of the woman who testified, "He told me everything I have done." (John 4:4-39)

"I know that you are descendants of Abraham. But you are trying to kill me, because my word has no room among you. I tell you what I have seen in the Father's presence; then do what you have heard from the Father." They answered and said to him, "Our father is Abraham." Jesus said to them, "If you were Abraham's children, you would be doing the works of Abraham. But now you are trying to kill me, a man who has told you the truth that I heard from God; Abraham did not do this. You are doing the works of your father!" They said to him, "We are not illegitimate. We have one Father, God."

Jesus said to them, "If God were your Father, you would love me, for I came from God and am here; I did not come on my own, but he sent me. Why do you not understand what I am saying? Because you cannot bear to hear my word. You belong to your father the devil and you willingly carry out your father's desires. He was a murderer from the beginning and does not stand in truth, because there is no truth in him. When he tells a lie, he speaks in character, because he is a liar and the father of lies. But because I speak the truth, you do not believe me. Can any of you charge me with sin? If I am telling the truth, why do you not believe me? Whoever belongs to God hears the words of God; for this reason you do not listen, because you do not belong to God." The Jews answered and said to him, "Are we not right in saying that you are a Samaritan and are possessed?"

Jesus answered, "I am not possessed; I honor my Father, but you dishonor me. I do not seek my own glory; there is one who seeks it and he is the one who judges. Amen, amen, I say to you, whoever keeps my word will never see death." So the Jews said to him, "Now we are sure that you are possessed. Abraham died, as did the prophets, yet you say, 'Whoever keeps my word will never taste death.' Are you greater than our father Abraham, who died? Or the prophets, who died? Who do you make yourself out to be?" Jesus answered, "If I glorify myself, my glory is worth nothing; but it is my Father who glorifies me, of whom you say, 'He is our God.' You do not know him, but I know him. And if I should say that I do not know him, I would be like you a liar. But I do know him and I keep his word. Abraham your father rejoiced to see my day; he saw it and was glad. So the Jews said to him, "You are not yet fifty years old and you have seen Abraham?" Jesus said to them, "Amen, amen, I say to you, before Abraham came to be, I AM." So they picked up stones to throw at him; but Jesus hid and went out of the temple area. (John 8:37-59)

As he passed by he saw a man blind from birth. His disciples asked him, "Rabbi, who sinned, this man or his parents, that he was born blind?" Jesus answered, "Neither he nor his parents sinned; it is so that the works of God might be made visible through him. We have to do the works of the one who sent me while it is day. Night is coming when no one can work. While I am in the world, I am the light of the world." When he had said this, he spat on the ground and made clay with the saliva, and smeared the clay on his eyes, and said to him, "Go wash in the Pool of Siloam" (which means Sent). So he went and washed, and came back able to see.

His neighbors and those who had seen him earlier as a beggar said, "Isn't this the one who used to sit and beg?" Some said, "It is," but others said, "No, he just looks like him." He said, "I am." So they said to him, "So how were your eyes opened?" He replied, "The man called Jesus made clay and anointed my eyes and told me, 'Go to Siloam and wash.' So I went there and washed and was able to see." And they said to him, "Where is he?" He said, "I don't know."

They brought the one who was once blind to the Pharisees. Now Jesus had made clay and opened his eyes on a sabbath. So then the Pharisees also asked him how he was able to see. He said to them, "He put clay on my eyes, and I washed, and now I can see." So some of the Pharisees said, "This man is not from God, because he does not keep the sabbath." But others said, "How can a sinful man do such signs?" And there was a division among them. So they said to the blind man again, "What do you have to say about him, since he opened your eyes?" He said, "He is a prophet." Now the Jews did not believe that he had been blind and gained his sight until they summoned the parents of the one who had gained his sight. They asked them, "Is this your son, who you say was born blind? How does he now see?" His parents answered and said, "We know that this is our son and that he was born blind. We do not know how he sees now, nor do we know who opened his eyes. Ask him, he is of age; he can speak for himself." His parents said this because they were afraid of the Jews, for the Jews had already agreed that if anyone acknowledged him as the Messiah, he would be expelled from the synagogue. For this reason his parents said, "He is of age; question him." So a second time they called the man who had been blind and said to him, "Give God the praise! We know that this man is a sinner." He replied, "If he is a sinner, I do not know. One thing I do know is that I was blind and now I see." So they said to him, "What did he do to you? How did he open your eyes?" He answered them, "I told you already and you did not listen. Why do you want to hear it again? Do you want to become his disciples, too?" They ridiculed him and said, "You are that man's disciple; we are disciples of Moses! We know that God spoke to Moses, but we do not know where this one is from." The man answered and said to them, "This is what is so amazing, that you do not know where he is from, yet he opened my eyes. We know that God does not listen to sinners, but if one is devout and does his will, he listens to him. It is unheard of that anyone ever opened the eyes of a person born blind. If this man were not from God, he would not be able to do anything." They answered and said to him, "You were born totally in sin, and are you trying to teach us?" Then they threw him out.

When Jesus heard that they had thrown him out, he found him and said, "Do you believe in the Son of Man?" He answered and said, "Who is he, sir, that I may believe in him?" Jesus said to him, "You have seen him and the one speaking with you is he." He said, "I do believe, Lord," and he worshipped him. Then Jesus said, "I came into this world for judgment, so that those who do not see might see, and those who do see might become blind." Some of the Pharisees who were with him heard this and said to him, "Surely we are not also blind, are we?" Jesus said to them, "If you were blind, you would have no sin; but now you are saying, 'We see,' so your sin remains." (John 9:1-41)

When Jesus arrived, he found that Lazarus had already been in the tomb for four days. Now Bethany was near Jerusalem, only about two miles away. And many of the Jews had come to Martha and Mary to comfort them about their brother. When Martha heard that Jesus was coming, she went to meet him; but Mary sat at home. Martha said to Jesus, "Lord, if you had been here, my brother would not have died. But even now I know that whatever you ask of God, God will give you." Jesus said to her, "Your brother will rise." Martha said to him, "I know he will rise, in the resurrection on the last day." Jesus told her, "I am the resurrection and the life; whoever believes in me, even if he dies, will live, and everyone who lives and believes in me will never die. Do you believe this?" She said to him, "Yes, Lord. I have come to believe that you are the Messiah, the Son of God, the one who is coming into the world." When she had said this, she went and called her sister Mary secretly, saying, "The teacher is here and is asking for you." As soon as she heard this, she rose quickly and went to him. For Jesus had not yet come into the village, but was still where Martha had met him. So when the Jews who were with her in the house comforting her saw Mary get up quickly and go out, they followed her, presuming that she was going to the tomb to weep there.

When Mary came to where Jesus was and saw him, she fell at his feet and said to him, "Lord, if you had been here, my brother would not have died." When Jesus saw her weeping and the Jews who had come with her weeping, he became perturbed and deeply troubled, and said, "Where have you laid him?" They said to him, "Sir, come and see." And Jesus wept. So the Jews said, "See how he loved him." But some of them said, "Could not the one who opened the eyes of the blind man have done something so that this man would not have died?"

So Jesus, perturbed again, came to the tomb. It was a cave, and a stone lay across it. Jesus said, "Take away the stone." Martha, the dead man's sister, said to him, "Lord, by now there will be a stench; he has been dead for four days." Jesus said to her, "Did I not tell you that if you believe you will see the glory of God?"

So they took away the stone. And Jesus raised his eyes and said, "Father, I thank you for hearing me. I know that you always hear me; but because of the crowd here I have said this, that they may believe that you sent me."

And when he had said this, he cried out in a loud voice, "Lazarus, come out!" The dead man came out, tied hand and foot with burial bands, and his face was wrapped in a cloth. So Jesus said to them, "Untie him and let him go." (John 11:17-44)

The child Jesus has grown up, the light of Epiphany now imposes itself on the streets, a light which responds to, which opposes itself to the expression of human affirmation in politics, in the common mentality, and in power.

Let us ask ourselves if we find ourselves in front of this figure, this reality, this person, if this You is in us, if this You invades our personality, if this You goes to our depths as a direction, as understanding, will, desire, love, if our life is this love.

Otherwise, we are standing on the flesh, and "all flesh is like grass, and all its glory like the flower of the field; the grass withers, and the flower wilts; but the word of the Lord remains forever" (1 Peter 1:24-25). This Word is not a discourse—it is a real person, a man, Jesus Christ.

Let us bring out the awareness of this presence from the depth of the fog, from misunderstanding, from all the dissonance. Let us recollect ourselves in front of the One to whom our life is a response, who is the foundation, the meaning of our personal responsibility.

We must quickly grasp once again this You whose presence the Gospels of Lent bring to our inner eye, to our imagination, making it easier to recognize the miracle of our life. The miracle of this presence is not given to those who do not recognize Him as their own, sufficient to define the very meaning, the very substance of life, to become their very name (1 Peter 2:6-8).

This You and this presence signal a change in our life. Therefore, Lent is the time of conversion. It is no longer a vague expectation, no longer a joy without responsibility because the announcement has just been given, of wonder at its initial manifestation. In front of this mature, strong manifestation—which tells us the scope for which he came ("Before Abraham was, I AM" [John 8:58])—in front of this mature presence that no longer hides the aims for which he came: to possess our lives—we must respond (Romans 8:2-23).

The first fundamental change that Lent brings, that the renewed awareness of this You should produce in our life, is that our life becomes a life of faith, becomes just—that is, lives by faith.

The time of God will enrich the time that passes—the time that becomes the time of faith will enrich our soul and comfort it, will make it always stronger, console it, make it fuller and more capable of joy.

"And those he predestined he also called; and those he called he also justified; and those he justified he also glorified" (Romans 8:30).

In short, it is a deep, radical change; it is holiness of life.

Lent is the time to change the criterion of value, the time of penitence. All the miracles of Lent were done to change people. The miracle of the fact that Jesus Christ revealed Himself in His mature personality, to propose Himself and attract our mature personality, aims to invade and transform us in Him.

This is the miracle by which others can glorify the Lord, the miracle by which people can understand that God has visited us, visits us: our transformation, our change.

A CHANGE IN US generates a place. The mature Christ, the newness of life that He brings, has created a new place, a new structure. And at the same time this new structure that our change produces becomes the place of the Spirit, becomes the objectivization of the power of the Spirit, as the Lord has done with the Church.

"Since you have purified yourselves by obedience to the truth for sincere mutual love, love one another intensely from a pure heart. You have been born anew, not from perishable but from imperishable seed, through the living and abiding word of God" (1 Peter 1:22-23).

God directs us to a new urgency of life: that our change may create a structure, because only this reveals Him as true, this creation not from a perishable seed, not from human will, not from the will of our own program, not from the will of our own refuge, not from the will of the one who flees from the earthly situation in which he has been placed to create his own earthly situation.

"Not from perishable but from imperishable seed, through the living and abiding word of God"—from being attracted, from having heard this Word, from this mature and strong Person who changes things (as with the Samaritan woman), which changes the man born blind, which changes death into life, which dominates things because "before Abraham was, I AM." I was there two thousand years ago, I am here now to encounter you, to call you, to sustain you. I want you.

Let us think again about the mature Jesus, the one who claims us, the one of whom the Gospels of Lent speak.

Let us think again about the change He brings: first of all a radical faith, from which we are born, and the hope that is a steadfast aspiration, and the charity that creates objective, new structures. This structure which is a miracle to all men, and first of all to us, because the Lord has visited and visits the world through us. And let us remind ourselves that the clearest action of this conversion in charity is obedience in its deepest, widest aspect, an obedience born not from a perishable seed, or for some other reason, but from an imperishable seed. "Behold, I am laying a stone in Zion, a cornerstone, chosen and precious, and whoever believes in it shall not be put to shame" (1 Peter 2:6).

Because the cornerstone without what rests on it—without the connection to Him—will remain a stumbling block. For us,

Jesus Christ can remain only a stumbling block if He does not become the one in whom all our life is supported.

It is the maturity of our person that corresponds, responds, adheres to the maturity of His person.

"Although you have not seen him you love him; even though you do not see him now yet believe in him, you rejoice with an indescribable and glorious joy, as you attain the goal of your faith, the salvation of your souls" (1 Peter 1:8).

The true theme of life has to do with our personhood. Everything begins from and returns there: the maturity of our person is the adhesion that we give to Jesus Christ in Lent.

This is the time when the Lord gathers us, saves us through the Word made flesh, who has become one of us. The liturgical year is the story of the Word of God in our life; Lent is the time of the Word of God that walks within the world.

But what other path can we walk with intelligence and freedom of heart if not the path that is clear and certain of its goal? Otherwise, it would be a place of violence. This is, in fact, the position of the person who seeks to bring salvation to the world through study, analysis, her own strength.

There is no clear and certain path if the ultimate image of this path is not a gift, a grace. There would only be the violent attempt to impose a goal.

The Christian path is often not clear and intelligent in us and is, instead, somehow unruly and resistant, obscure and almost gloomy, unsatisfied, because our personality is not dominated, invested, determined in its imagination, in its judgment, and in its heart by the "last day," by the end. *Love for the second coming*, love for the end of the world, love for the final manifestation—about which Saint Paul speaks in chapter 8 of the Letter to the Romans—has a particular name: *hope*. Christian hope is the certainty of the final outcome, the certainty in which we live our whole lives as love for a certain future.

"The end of all things is at hand. Therefore, be serious and sober in prayer" (1 Peter 4:7).

Prayer is the awareness of reality in its truth, and the truth of reality is Jesus Christ, the Word made flesh, in whom all things consist, because "the Father has given everything into His hands and, without Him, nothing came into being" (John 3:35; 1:3).

Prayer is, therefore, the awareness of the ultimate truth of things, Jesus Christ ("God the tenacious consistency of things"), and the truth of Christ will be manifested at His return, when everything will be fulfilled.

"I tell you, brothers, the time is running out. From now on, let those having wives act as not having them, those weeping as not weeping, those rejoicing as not rejoicing, those buying as not owning, those using the world as not using it fully. For the world in its present form is passing away" (1 Corinthians 7:29-31).

The sense of His coming, of the final manifestation, should become the determining content of our awareness, because at His return we will be fully ourselves: "His return" is the coming to being of "ourselves."

Therefore, the Saints aspired to see Him. They longed for death, just like each of us links our good or bad mood to the hope of certain events, because our awareness is dominated by the events to which we aspire, by the imagination of the future we hypothesize.

The sign of how much the desire for His coming dominates in us is our sense of the time that passes quickly, the feeling of the ephemeral, of the provisional. This sense of the brevity of time brings about a cheerful recognition of the true equality of everything: to be married or not is the same thing. All things are equal because the consistency of them is not in the form but in their being a step toward His arrival, toward the Event. The consistency of each thing is in its final manifestation.

This is not a flattening or a monotony, though, because if one is married and the other is not, if one cries and another does not, all of it has to do with the design of the Father. This is the true equality: everything consists in what will come and therefore in the relationship of what exists to this coming.

To the cheerful sense of the brevity of time corresponds, as a corollary, the profound absence of worry, of anxiety. Anxiety and worry derive from the relationship of our own project to what must be done to bring about that project. A characteristic of worry and anxiety is the ease with which we compare ourselves with the other, from which come envy, jealousy, resentment.

During Lent, the first aspect of conversion, the *mea culpa*, the first gesture of contrition, should be placing ourselves in front of the desire for His final coming. No other attitude, by its nature, breaks out into a cry, into the pure prayer, "Come."

This is so true that the Book of Revelation ends by saying "Come," and the first prayer of the early Christians is "Come" (Revelation 22:17-20).

Moreover, this is the only attitude that makes us abandon everything, because, even though death still brings a sense of fear, it is in this fear that we need to abandon ourselves. We cannot become a total aspiration "for Him who comes" if not through love. Therefore, to forget everything is to have everything transformed into desire for Him.

> I consider that the sufferings of this present time are as nothing compared with the glory to be revealed for us. For creation awaits with eager expectation the revelation of the children of God; for creation was made subject to futility, not of its own accord but because of the one who subjected it, in hope that creation itself would be set free from slavery to corruption and share in the glorious freedom of the children of God. (Romans 8:18-21)

We are dealing with a different anthropology, of a human form radically different, even if it lives in the flesh, than all other men ("insofar as I now live in the flesh, I live by faith in the Son of God" [Galatians 2:20]).

WE CANNOT IN FACT pronounce the word "liberation" without feeling and trembling before the true value of this word: the desire for the second coming of Christ.

> We know that all creation is groaning in labor pains
> even until now; and not only that, but we ourselves, who
> have the first fruits of the Spirit, we also groan within
> ourselves as we wait for adoption, the redemption of our
> bodies. For in hope we were saved. Now hope that sees
> for itself is not hope. For who hopes for what one sees?
> But if we hope for what we do not see, we wait with
> *endurance.* (Romans 8:22-25)

This last word summarizes the ethic, the description of human behavior from the point of view of the relationship with reality, time and space, things and people, for men who live this faith in His return and walk *spe erecti* [upright with hope].

What does it mean that the time is short and yet we are cheerful, what does it mean that all things are equal because their consistence is in His coming, if not that life is governed by patience?

True patience is full of profound cheer and does not get worried: "By your perseverance you will secure your lives" (Luke 21:19). Patience, therefore, is the force of a tension toward His return; as Saint Catherine said, it is born from a cry: "The truth is like the light that is silent when it is time to be silent and, being silent, shouts with the shout of patience."

How does the Bible describe the second coming, the final manifestation of the Lord?

If Lent is the Word of God that walks in the world, then the last day will be that to which the Lenten journey leads: Easter. To know the terminology with which the Bible reveals the ultimate fulfillment of things means to go deeper into perceiving how the Lord—who speaks to us in the history of His Revelation—sees the relationship between our life and that day. To connect the relationship between our journey and that ultimate moment means to live a life dominated by the idea of the end. And living with the end in mind is the most synthetic and recapitulatory aspect of conversion. True contrition, in fact, is completely dominated by that final event.

The biblical terminology speaks of "fulfillment of the promises." The Hebrew story was the story of the promise, and the life of the Jewish people was the life of a promise. This unique story of the Jewish people was a sign that God had created for all of humanity, because man had been created as a promise, and human history is the story of this promise.

For this reason, in the Acts of the Apostles, when Saint Paul makes his speech to the Athenians, he says: "The God who made the world and all that is in it, the Lord of heaven and earth, does not dwell in sanctuaries made by human hands, nor is he served by human hands because he needs anything. Rather it is he who gives to everyone life and breath and everything. He made from one the whole human race to dwell on the entire surface of the earth, and he fixed the ordered seasons and the boundaries of their regions, so that people might seek God, even perhaps grope for him and find him, though indeed he is not far from any one of us" (Acts 17:24-27).

The movement of the human story, the story of civilization, has one unique aim: to seek God, because only He is the meaning of existence.

The fulfillment of the promises made to Abraham is Jesus Christ, and He will reveal that He is the answer to the promises in a complete way, unequivocally, manifestly, at His second coming.

In the Letter to the Galatians, Saint Paul says: "For through faith you are all children of God in Christ Jesus. For all of you who were baptized into Christ have clothed yourselves with Christ. There is neither Jew nor Greek, there is neither slave nor free person, there is not male and female; for you are all one in Christ Jesus. And if you belong to Christ, then you are Abraham's descendant, heirs according to the promise" (Galatians 3:26-29).

In chapter 15 of the Letter to the Romans (8-12), Saint Paul affirms: "For I say that Christ became a minister of the circumcised to show God's truthfulness, to confirm the promises to the patriarchs, but so that the Gentiles might glorify God for his mercy. As it is written: 'Therefore, I will praise you among the Gentiles and sing praises to your name.' And again it says: 'Rejoice, O Gentiles, with his people.' And again: 'Praise the Lord, all you Gentiles, and let all the peoples praise him.' And again Isaiah says: 'The root of Jesse shall come, raised up to rule the Gentiles; in him shall the Gentiles hope.'"

CHRIST, THEN, IS THE fulfillment of the promises, and this means that Christ is everything; and not just "in a manner of speaking," because it is not, first of all, our choice, but the recognition of a reality: "I am the cornerstone" (Psalm 118:22; Matthew 21:42). It is a given fact that He is the cornerstone upon which, alone, we can build.

> As God is faithful, our word to you is not "yes" and "no." For the Son of God, Jesus Christ, who was proclaimed to you by us, Silvanus and Timothy and me, was not "yes" and "no," but "yes" has been in Him. For however many are the promises of God, their Yes is in him; therefore, the Amen from us also goes through him to God for glory. But the one who gives us security with you in Christ and who anointed us is God; he has also put his seal upon us and given the Spirit in our hearts as a first installment (2 Corinthians 1:18-22).

Christ is defined as the "yes," but this "amen" has been spoken, is already present among us.

So, if history is nothing other than the mysterious development of this presence until His final triumph, the sensation that we should have of the human time in which we participate is that of being taken by this fact that, like a rushing torrent, is overwhelming us and carrying us toward the finish line—it is being within what has already happened, it is time as memory.

Saint Paul, speaking of Christian existence, uses the term *redimentes tempus*, redeeming the time (Ephesians 5:16). "To redeem" means to make time true, to make its value come to light in time. All the other terms—to liberate, to make useful, constructive, edifying, positive—are analogous.

Saint Paul wrote: "Therefore, the 'amen' from us also goes through him to God for glory" (2 Corinthians 1:20).

In the measure in which we are aware of this definitive and total belonging to Jesus Christ, we have the presentiment of living the end, we anticipate what will happen.

The feeling or the awareness that defines the Christian is the expectation of His second coming: this alone transfigures our face.

Only if we feel ourselves captivated by the "yes" that Christ is—"For all of you who were baptized into Christ have clothed yourselves with Christ" (Galatians 3:27)—does the feeling of "Come, Lord" develop itself in us as the dominant feeling of life, and our expression begins to be "amen," "yes."

This means that in prosperity or adversity, in the good and the bad, in pain and in joy, one begins to feel that everything is "yes," that everything is fulfilling itself and *non est illis scandalum* (Psalm 119:165, Vulgate), there is no longer any scandal.

We can have a similar awareness of ourselves only within the fact of Christ, therefore within the communion with all those of whom Christ is made.

"But the one who gives us security with you in Christ and who anointed us is God" (2 Corinthians 1:21)—that is, chosen and consecrated; Jesus is the Christ, the Anointed of God, who has united us with Himself, chosen us as part of Himself.

BUT THIS PASSAGE FROM Saint Paul should say something more to us: "He *has also put his seal upon us* and given the Spirit in our hearts as a first installment" (2 Corinthians 1:22).

The word *seal*, in the full awareness of the history of Christian doctrine, signifies a change in our ontology.

God is the creator, and when He moves He touches our being. The seal therefore is the outcome of the redemptive and recreative power of God, which transforms our being, and in fact transforms us into His "yes."

But how does God put His seal upon our hearts? With an event that is recognizable as a gesture in our personal history, with the *sacrament*. The sacrament is the gesture with which Christ seizes our being and changes it, giving it a different form.

Chapter 3 of the Letter to the Galatians (26-27) says: "For through faith you are all children of God in Christ Jesus. For all of you who were baptized into Christ have clothed yourselves with Christ": you are the beginning of the fulfillment, you are the "yes." Through the sacrament the "yes" and "amen" which is Christ—the "already present" of the final fulfillment—engages us in our depths. Therefore in the sacrament memory deepens and thus the feeling of His coming becomes ever more powerful and life is transformed. Life in fact is transformed not because we compare our conscience with the moral law but because of these events that happen.

In the sacrament, we are involved in the "already" of Christ, we are involved in the "yes" that is already among us, in the history of this presence that is overwhelming everything, time and space, toward His final manifestation. The sacrament is the gesture with which Christ takes us again and again and brings us always more "within."

In the last chapter of the Book of Revelation, the word "Come" persists as an aspiration for the beloved and truly marks the physiognomy that should always be ours: but that word is realized in the sacramental gesture, through the infallible awareness of the bride of Christ, the Church.

The sacrament is the gesture with which Christ brings our personality most profoundly into Himself. The sacramental life—Penance in particular, which is the second Baptism, and the Eucharist—has as its pale human comparison the example of a person who is distracted and does not recognize the presence of someone he loves, and that beloved person puts a hand on his shoulder saying, "I am here." It is another world that happens in that moment between those people; it is a new awareness of self, a new consciousness of a relationship with time and with things.

"God has also put his seal upon us and given the Spirit in our hearts as a first installment" (2 Corinthians 1:22).

"He has given the Spirit in our hearts as a first installment" means to have the presentiment of the end, to begin to feel the light of the end. In the sacramental life, more than in any other moment, we have the installment of the Spirit, we begin to understand what is the unity of the world (Romans 8), that all is good, that we are one thing only, that Christ is the Lord.

In the Letter to the Ephesians (6:17), Saint Paul says that the sword of the Spirit is the word of God.

We have said that Lent is the Word of God that walks in the world—that is, a sword that cuts (Hebrews 4:12): the Word of God generates division and conflict. This is the meaning of the word mortification as the law of Christian life. The Word of God is meant to bring life, and yet it cuts and divides: death and resurrection.

The condition of resurrection is death; the condition of life passes through death.

In chapter 8 of the Letter to the Romans (verse 2), Saint Paul says: "For the law of the spirit of life in Christ Jesus has freed you from the law of sin and death."

Therefore, there is a contrast, there is an alternative to the Word of God: the law of sin and death.

In chapter 2 of the First Letter to the Corinthians (12-13), Saint Paul says again: "We have not received the spirit of the world but the Spirit that is from God, so that we may understand the things freely given us by God. And we speak about them not with words taught by human wisdom, but with words taught by the Spirit, describing spiritual realities in spiritual terms."

Thus, in the Second Letter to the Corinthians (10:3-4), Saint Paul says: "For, although we are in the flesh [among all the things that we do], we do not battle according to the flesh, for the weapons of our battle are not of flesh but are enormously powerful, capable of destroying fortresses."

The Word of God is a sword because it fights, and if it fights, it wins, because it destroys fortresses, that is, it destroys even the positions that have been built through centuries and millennia, all the way to original sin, in us. It destroys even the positions that constitute the dominant culture, all of our personal and social habits. The Word of God cannot but be felt as a sword of the Spirit, and the Spirit is the one who creates, the one who redeems, the redemptive power of Christ.

The Spirit creates, sanctifies, redeems, builds by seeming to demolish, demolishing in fact our human bones, demolishing our human walls.

WHAT IS OPPOSED to the Word of God as the sword of the Spirit? Everything in us that tends not to be converted, not to be of Christ, that seeks to be autonomous.

Such illusory autonomy can derive from pride or from infidelity, from a lack of faith, from a lack of the sense of the mystery of Christ. Autonomy as self-love would like to put its own reactions as the measure of its actions and, thus, of its relationships. From this come envy, jealousy, fights, recriminations, dissatisfaction, while the criterion should be the event of Christ and the expectation of His return.

But the true evil root that opposes itself to the sword of the Spirit and does not allow this sword to break us in contrition, the true root is the lack of a sense of the mystery of Christ: history and existence should be valued on the basis of the mystery of Christ and not on the basis of our times and our rhythms—that is, on our demands.

All things are equally fragile: this means that the consistency of all things is a mystery, is His death and resurrection, His second coming. The consistency of things is not in what we make, because the truth of things acts hiddenly, that is, supernaturally. Things are made according to a work that is within, in the depths, in truth.

Autonomy, which derives from infidelity, has a very clear symptom: the gestures of each day, the relationships with people happen outside of the sentiment of the end or the memory of Christ. If our life manages to have some unity, this unity comes from the outside, from the force of will, in a way that is abstract, in the best of cases, moralistic. This effort is exhausting.

Christ accepted from the Father that the redemptive strength He had within Him played out slowly and hiddenly through millennia of history, whereas He could have brought it about in a single moment. Christ accepted from the Father that He remain in Palestine, while the people who would have accepted Him better were in Tyre and Sidon, in the lands of the pagans; Christ accepted to be crucified in the time fixed by the Father; and so we do not accept the history of Christ if we get scandalized because we do not see in what sense our heavy and opaque concerns have eternal meaning within His coming or within the mystery of His death and resurrection. This is faith: to believe that within what we do there is the mystery of His coming.

If the memory of Christ and the expectation of His coming are in us, and so in everything, the clearness of the transfiguration begins, the presentiment begins, even while remaining opaque and heavy (because it is in this enigma that faith lives). What begins to be felt in the Eucharist begins to be felt in everything that is born from us.

Even if we believe in the second coming of Christ, in the memory of Christ, even if we accept the faith truly, we remain unsatisfied and in a certain inquietude because things are still not like they will be at His coming, things are still not as we would like them to be for our happiness. But Christ came to die—He came, that is, to break through the surface of these things, but He breaks through in a mysterious history.

Things are still heavy and opaque: we cannot expect our peace from the fact that these things change, but from our change we can expect the transfiguration of these things, according to the mysterious design of the Father, in patience.

If, at a certain point, our gaze and our heart truly change things, this is a miracle that God does when He wants. In patience the Spirit will not hold back His testimony which is necessary for the faith to be reasonable.

But when one of our actions becomes a miracle—that is, when it is seen as part of the sign of Christ—then we are already detached from it, we see it as small, we no longer are slaves to it, and our happiness does not depend anymore on the outcome itself. Christ died without seeing things change, and thus, each of us is destined to live the same trajectory of Christ and to die as if we have not accomplished anything. If the Father treated the Master like this, He will also treat His disciples like this.

It is normal that the outcome of our actions do not correspond to that aspiration that in a creaturely way we have within, that they do not correspond to the desire for happiness, fullness, satisfaction. It seems like a failure, but it is not; faith makes us understand this and therefore makes us "live together steadfast in Christ and in joy."

Our faith should become greater, because we should carry the gravity and opacity of things in the certainty that Christ is there and that through these things, just as they are, His second and definitive coming happens (*Parousia*), His return happens.

Things are heavy, but we carry them, because we are made like Christ, the giant who runs the race.[14]

Chapter 4

EASTER

SAINT PAUL TRAVELED THROUGH the whole known world of his time: he faced persecutions, shipwrecks; "night and day, I unceasingly admonished each of you with tears" (Acts 20:31). What could have given him the courage, the strength to face reality with his faith, to act as he did? He was living from what he had experienced. What gave meaning to his life?

There exists an anxiety in the heart of man: it is the expectation of life even in the condition of death. Despite his progress, his good will, his dominion over the things of this world, man still has to die. Outside of ourselves, we recognize that life is diminishing all the time. The idea of an immense effort, that would be able to animate and liberate humanity, is not a solution, if there is not the announcement that the dominion of death has been destroyed, that the true enemy of man has been overcome (1 Corinthians 15:26).

Our deepest obligation is to go to what is fundamental, radical in life.

Death is the source of disintegration, that which puts itself between man and his fulfillment. Christ has overcome death: all of humanity can look with trust to that first man who overcame death.

What moved Paul, what gave meaning to his work, was a new hope.

This is how we understand the gathering of people around Jesus: communion in the name of hope—the hope of overcoming death, the victory over death.

The victory of Christ is His resurrection. "And if Christ has not been raised, then empty (too) is our preaching; empty, too, your faith" (1 Corinthians 15:14).

If there is any motive other than this, it is vain, invalid: stirring ourselves up would be vain and without result.

This is the definitive announcement: nothing beyond this can be announced. The world must keep going toward its fulfillment, but the definitive has already happened: this hope calls us and makes us different from the world.

No man is capable of this announcement. Only by the grace of God is Paul what he is, and it is the same for every Christian. Only in this way can we affirm that the Gospel which is announced, which others receive, is salvation. It is salvation because Christ is risen. We are only able to announce that Christ is risen.

We are witnesses to the resurrection of Christ.

If we preach, if we speak, the point on which the problem of believing or of not believing stands is that Christ is risen from the dead.

If Christ were not risen and, thus, if we will not rise, everything would fall, preaching and faith would be in vain.

We may be the most miserable men in the world, but what defines us is faith in Christ, in this world (1 Corinthians 15:12-19). In this way, we attain the resurrection.

By virtue of one man, death came, but Christ has overcome evil: He has conquered the powers, the principalities, the powers of the air (Ephesians 1:15-2:5).

And the last enemy to be definitively destroyed in each of us and in the world will be death, when Jesus Christ will return.

We will expose ourselves to dangers, to fatigue, not for a certain advantage, but in order to be witnesses to the risen Christ.

What brings comfort to our labor, to our courage in spending everything, is the fact that life in Christ does not fail.

We can accept death only because of this hope, only because death has been defeated.

There are no longer difficult situations or failures: the blind see, the crippled and lame walk. Even for them, there is hope.

Life will no longer fail, and there is no other name from which we can have life, only Christ (Acts 4:12).

To make the world a better place, to overcome contradictions, to create better structures—these are the strength and the effort of a splendid humanism, but in themselves, they do not qualify as the work of Christians. This work has a radical point that is its end and active characteristic: Jesus Christ, risen.

In this sense, Christian discourse is totally new, irreducible to the discourse of a simple social or civil advancement: whoever is humanly alive, authentic, honest can speak about social justice, peace, racism, and the contradictions of the Third World. Even we can speak that way, and rightly so: but what makes the essence of our attitude new is the foundation that Christ is risen. In the Holy Scriptures, this clash between humanism and Christ is clearly expressed in the discourse of Paul at the Areopagus in Athens.

> While Paul was waiting for them in Athens, he grew exasperated at the sight of the city full of idols. So he debated in the synagogue with the Jews and with the worshipers, and daily in the public square with whoever happened to be there. Even some of the Epicurean and Stoic philosophers engaged him in discussion. Some asked, "What is this scavenger trying to say?" Others said, "He sounds like a promoter of foreign deities," because he was preaching about "Jesus" and "Resurrection." They took him and led him to the Areopagus and said, "May we learn what this new teaching is that you speak of? For you bring some strange notions to our ears; we should like to know what these things mean." Now all the Athenians as well as the foreigners residing there used their time for nothing else but telling or hearing something new.
>
> Then Paul stood up at the Areopagus and said: "You Athenians, I see that in every respect you are very religious. For as I walked around looking carefully at your

shrines, I even discovered an altar inscribed, 'To an Unknown God.' What therefore you unknowingly worship, I proclaim to you. The God who made the world and all that is in it, the Lord of heaven and earth, does not dwell in sanctuaries made by human hands, nor is he served by human hands because he needs anything. Rather it is he who gives to everyone life and breath and everything. He made from one the whole human race to dwell on the entire surface of the earth, and he fixed the ordered seasons and the boundaries of their regions, so that people might seek God, even perhaps grope for him and find him, though indeed he is not far from any one of us. For 'In him we live and move and have our being,' as even some of your poets have said, 'For we too are his offspring.' Since therefore we are the offspring of God, we ought not to think that the divinity is like an image fashioned from gold, silver, or stone by human art and imagination. God has overlooked the times of ignorance, but now he demands that all people everywhere repent because he has established a day on which he will 'judge the world with justice' through a man he has appointed, and he has provided confirmation for all by raising him from the dead." When they heard about resurrection of the dead, some began to scoff, but others said, "We should like to hear you on this some other time." And so Paul left them. But some did join him, and became believers. Among them were Dionysius, a member of the Court of the Areopagus, a woman named Damaris, and others with them. (Acts 17:16-34)

The people listen to Paul with attention during the whole first part of his speech to the Athenians, men who were imbued with classical humanism and expressive of a certain type of effort of human knowledge, but when he announces the central point of the Gospel, which is Christ risen, they tell him to come back another day. In order to see another sign of the difference between Christ and humanism, we can compare the death of Socrates with the death of Christ.

Before his death, Socrates is serene, aware, he comforts his disciples, he can now liberate himself from the weight of the body: death is his friend because it frees him from the yoke.

Christ is scared (see the Passion of Matthew 26:36 ff.), He is afraid, *maestus est*. He seeks the comfort of his disciples, He asks them to stay with him, to pray. He is upset, He feels abandoned, He asks for help from the Father: Father, free me from this supreme, definitive hour. He accepts the cross at the conclusion of a supreme combat: a final cry.

Socrates escapes this world, this irremediable situation. He has the hope of the one who does not hope, a life with no possibility of recovery: he flees, he runs away from life, from this condition.

Christ engages in total combat with death: redemption is suffered in full desolation. He accepts entering the kingdom of death in order to conquer it.

This situation of death and sin is redeemable and recoverable. It is here that every simply human discourse diverges from the fully human discourse, that is, the Christian one: no man can expect victory for himself over death, no man can create it for himself, only God can give man this victory.

But the Athenians in the Areopagus reject this announcement as folly.

Paul's preaching is the announcement of a judgment on the whole world, in front of which and for which we are called to be witnesses to the resurrection of Christ.

This is the point where every falsehood falls: faith in Christ must be the light of truth over everything.

IF IT IS TRUTH, THOUGH, that the ultimate depth of the claim of faith is faith in Christ risen, then all action, the whole Christian dynamic, must derive from this its criterion of authenticity.

And, in the first place, let us reflect on the fact that, if Jesus emerges as the ultimate judge, as the only one who has overcome death, the only hope for man is that everything be rebuilt, remade, recapitulated, called together, subjected in Him and to Him, so that He can hand it over to the Father and God may be all in all.

This is the establishment of unity in Christ.

If sin sets the stage for disintegration and leads to death, to confusion, to disorder, by which the world comes to nothing, it is clear that everything must be rebuilt in unity with Christ Jesus: the unmistakable paradigm.

The Church is the place that announces this foundational unity of the world, the place where Christ is announced.

It is the place of communication where salvation can come. Through the unity of the one who creates the unity of the world, that is, Christ and His Church, the unity of the world is rebuilt in everything and everyone.

Here then, the word *communion* emerges as the unity among us, which is the place of the new world, recapitulated in Christ.

This implies the necessity of a visible place in which the unity around Christ can be built.

The unity of the spirit in the bond of peace is the one true hope, the actualization of Baptism.

> Therefore, remember that at one time you, Gentiles in the flesh, called the uncircumcision by those called the circumcision, which is done in the flesh by human hands, were at that time without Christ, alienated from the community of Israel and strangers to the covenants of promise, without hope and without God in the world. But now in Christ Jesus you who once were far off have become near by the blood of Christ. For he is our peace, he who made both one and broke down the dividing wall of enmity, through his flesh, abolishing the law with its commandments and legal claims, that he might create in himself one new person in place of the two, thus establishing peace, and might reconcile both with God, in one body, through the cross, putting that enmity to death by it. He came and preached peace to you who were far off and peace to those who were near, for through him we both have access in one Spirit to the Father. So then you are no longer strangers and sojourners, but you are fellow citizens with the holy ones and members of the household of God, built upon the foundation of the apostles and prophets, with Christ Jesus himself as the capstone.

Through him the whole structure is held together and grows into a temple sacred in the Lord; in him you also are being built together into a dwelling place of God in the Spirit. (Ephesians 2:11-22)

The fundamental work is to labor in building up the unity of the body of Christ—with the visible structure of the body of Christ. From this unity that is realized in the body of Christ follows—in our commitment to live the faith—the experience of a vast network of relationships that are always more permeated by communion. We see, for example, the change in life that the first Christian communities experienced.

You were dead in your transgressions and sins in which you once lived following the age of this world, following the ruler of the power of the air, the spirit that is now at work in the disobedient. All of us once lived among them in the desires of our flesh, following the wishes of the flesh and the impulses, and we were by nature children of wrath, like the rest. But God, who is rich in mercy, because of the great love he had for us, even when we were dead in our transgressions, brought us to life with Christ (by grace you have been saved), raised us up with him, and seated us with him in the heavens in Christ Jesus. (Ephesians 2:1-6)

Wives should be subordinate to their husbands as to the Lord. For the husband is head of his wife just as Christ is head of the church, he himself the savior of the body. As the church is subordinate to Christ, so wives should be subordinate to their husbands in everything. Husbands, love your wives, even as Christ loved the church and handed himself over for her to sanctify her, cleansing her by the bath of water with the word, that he might present to himself the church in splendor, without spot or wrinkle or any such thing, that she might be holy and without blemish. So [also] husbands should love their wives as their own bodies. He who loves his wife loves himself. For no one hates his own flesh but rather nourishes and cherishes it, even as Christ does the church, because we are members of his body. "For this reason a man shall leave [his] father and [his] mother and be joined to his wife, and the two shall become one flesh." This is a great mystery, but I speak in reference to Christ and the church. In any case, each one of you should love his wife as himself, and the wife should respect her husband. (Ephesians 5:22-33)

Children, obey your parents [in the Lord], for this is right. "Honor your father and mother." This is the first commandment with a promise, "that it may go well with you and that you may have a long life on earth." Fathers, do not provoke your children to anger, but bring them up with the training and instruction of the Lord. Slaves, be obedient to your human masters with fear and trembling, in sincerity of heart, as to Christ, not only when being watched, as currying favor, but as slaves of Christ, doing the will of God from the heart, willingly serving the Lord and not human beings, knowing that each will be requited from the Lord for whatever good he does, whether he is slave or free. Masters, act in the same way toward them, and stop bullying, knowing that both they and you have a Master in heaven and that with him there is no partiality. (Ephesians 6:1-9)

My brothers, show no partiality as you adhere to the faith in our glorious Lord Jesus Christ. For if a man with gold rings on his fingers and in fine clothes comes into your assembly, and a poor person in shabby clothes also comes in, and you pay attention to the one wearing the fine clothes and say, "Sit here, please," while you say to the poor one, "Stand there," or "Sit at my feet," have you not made distinctions among yourselves and become judges with evil designs? Listen, my beloved brothers. Did not God choose those who are poor in the world to be rich in faith and heirs of the kingdom that he promised to those who love him? But you dishonored the poor person. Are not the rich oppressing you? And do they themselves not haul you off to court? Is it not they who blaspheme the noble name that was invoked over you? However, if you fulfill the royal law according to the scripture, "You shall love your neighbor as yourself," you are doing well. But if you show partiality, you commit sin, and are convicted by the law as transgressors. For whoever keeps the whole law, but falls short in one particular, has become guilty in respect to all of it. For he who said, "You shall not commit adultery," also said, "You shall not kill." Even if you do not commit adultery but kill, you have become a transgressor of the law. So speak and so act as people who will be judged by the law of freedom. For the judgment is merciless to one who has not shown mercy; mercy triumphs over judgment. (James 2:1-13)

The community of believers was of one heart and mind, and no one claimed that any of his possessions was his own, but they had everything in common. With great power the apostles bore witness to the resurrection of the Lord Jesus, and great favor was accorded them all. There was no needy person among them, for those who owned property or houses would sell them, bring the proceeds of the sale, and put them at the feet of the apostles, and they were distributed to each according to need. (Acts 4:32-35)

Above all, though, we must understand and live the connection of everything with the foundation that is Christ risen from the dead.

Chapter 5

ASCENSION

ON THE OCCASION OF the Ascension, the Church invites us to reflect on a paradox. It is a feast, and yet it commemorates the abandonment of men on the part of Christ.

The disciples are sad, but Christ has said, "It is better for you that I go. For if I do not go, the Advocate will not come to you" (John 16:7): our faith cannot be lived except through the *absence* of manifestations of the power of Christ according to our expectation. Absence: the canceling of the strength, the canceling of the sense of superiority and greatness, the annulment of the miracle in the strict sense of the word.

Our Christian vocation does not become authentic except in this absence. As long as Christ was present, the action of Christianity in the world was the action of His person, the vocation of the apostles was in the shadow of His person.

Where Christ exists no longer in terms of personally visible action, then His action coincides, is identified, with the motivations and work of our person.

The phenomenon that unites us to God in this absence is *prayer*, as the height of self-forgetfulness, which is asking in the name of Christ, that is, asking for His kingdom to come.

> Then Jesus approached and said to them, "All power in heaven and on earth has been given to me. Go, therefore, and make disciples of all nations, baptizing them in the name of the Father, and of the Son, and of the holy

Spirit, teaching them to observe all that I have commanded you. And behold, I am with you always, until the end of the age." (Matthew 28:18-20; Mark 15:14-18)

He said to them, "These are my words that I spoke to you while I was still with you, that everything written about me in the law of Moses and in the prophets and psalms must be fulfilled." Then he opened their minds to understand the scriptures. And he said to them, "Thus it is written that the Messiah would suffer and rise from the dead on the third day and that repentance, for the forgiveness of sins, would be preached in his name to all the nations, beginning from Jerusalem. You are witnesses of these things. And [behold] I am sending the promise of my Father upon you; but stay in the city until you are clothed with power from on high." Then he led them [out] as far as Bethany, raised his hands, and blessed them. As he blessed them he parted from them and was taken up to heaven. They did him homage and then returned to Jerusalem with great joy, and they were continually in the temple praising God. (Luke 24:44-53)

When did the Apostles understand their vocation? They were together with him for three years and didn't understand!

"I have told you this while I am with you. The Advocate, the holy Spirit that the Father will send in my name—he will teach you everything and remind you of all that I told you" (John 14:25-26). "But I tell you the truth, it is better for you that I go. For if I do not go, the Advocate will not come to you. But if I go, I will send him to you" (John 16:7).

The Ascension is thus the beginning of Pentecost. The thunder of Pentecost for the attentive and vibrating soul is already in the Ascension and is expected from afar.

The Apostles understood who they were, what that irreversible fact of their call was destined to, on the day of Pentecost.

How deep and how full of security, of joy and gratitude, it is to feel our own person being put together again, to feel the rebuilding of the world in the continual recovery of certain truths, certain words, certain values.

As it is written, "What eye has not seen, and ear has not heard . . . God has prepared for those who love him" (1 Corinthians 2:9).

> God has revealed this to us through the Spirit. For the Spirit scrutinizes everything, even the depths of God. Among human beings, who knows what pertains to a person except the spirit of the person that is within? Similarly, no one knows what pertains to God except the Spirit of God. We have not received the spirit of the world but the Spirit that is from God, so that we may understand the things freely given us by God. And we speak about them not with words taught by human wisdom, but with words taught by the Spirit, describing spiritual realities in spiritual terms. Now the natural person does not accept what pertains to the Spirit of God, for to him it is foolishness, and he cannot understand it, because it is judged spiritually. (1 Corinthians 2:10-14)

> For those who live according to the flesh are concerned with the things of the flesh, but those who live according to the spirit with the things of the spirit. The concern of the flesh is death, but the concern of the spirit is life and peace. For the concern of the flesh is hostility toward God; it does not submit to the law of God, nor can it; and those who are in the flesh cannot please God. But you are not in the flesh; on the contrary, you are in the spirit, if only the Spirit of God dwells in you. Whoever does not have the Spirit of Christ does not belong to him. But if Christ is in you, although the body is dead because of sin, the spirit is alive because of righteousness. If the Spirit of the one who raised Jesus from the dead dwells in you, the one who raised Christ from the dead will give life to your mortal bodies also, through his Spirit that dwells in you. (Romans 8:5-11)

The division that is in us will be overcome by means of his Spirit that dwells in us, completely overcome at the end, but also already overcome as a beginning, as an event.

> Consequently, brothers, we are not debtors to the flesh, to live according to the flesh. For if you live according

to the flesh, you will die, but if by the spirit you put to death the deeds of the body, you will live. For those who are led by the Spirit of God are children of God. For you did not receive a spirit of slavery to fall back into fear, but you received a spirit of adoption, through which we cry, "Abba, Father!" The Spirit itself bears witness with our spirit that we are children of God, and if children, then heirs, heirs of God and joint heirs with Christ, if only we suffer with him so that we may also be glorified with him. (Romans 8:12-17)

In the same way, the Spirit too comes to the aid of our weakness; for we do not know how to pray as we ought, but the Spirit itself intercedes with inexpressible groanings. And the one who searches hearts knows what is the intention of the Spirit, because it intercedes for the holy ones according to God's will. (Romans 8:26-27)

"But now I am going to the one who sent me, and not one of you asks me, 'Where are you going?'" (John 16:5). It is the question we ask when things seem to escape us, and they seem to escape us when memory is no longer memory, when memory is diminished. "But because I told you this, grief has filled your hearts" (John 16:6). It is this grief that saves the Apostles, because it was the indicator that in their heart and in their body there was an attachment to Christ, even if they did not understand anything.

"But I tell you the truth, it is better for you that I go. For if I do not go, the Advocate will not come to you. But if I go, I will send him to you" (John 16:7). You will not become adults, you will no longer reach the autonomy of your personality, unless the Spirit ensures these things when he is knowingly accepted, requested, invoked by you.

I have much more to tell you, but you cannot bear it now. But when he comes, the Spirit of truth, he will guide you to all truth. He will not speak on his own, but he will speak what he hears, and will declare to you the things that are coming. He will glorify me, because he will take from what is mine and declare it to you. Everything that the Father has is mine; for this reason I told you that he will take from what is mine and declare it to you. (John 16:12-15)

Let us meditate on the Spirit that overshadows the womb of Our Lady, making her conceive: the new root of our being.

The Spirit indicates the real strength that penetrates us and changes us ontologically, changes our being, makes us new creatures, and thus the Spirit makes us understand, accomplishes the miracle. When he overshadowed the womb of the Virgin, she did not understand everything at once, so much so that the Gospel is full of Our Lady's questions, and even for her there will be a Pentecost, but it was a beginning just like it was in us, the beginning of an understanding without understanding. Our prayer must be a calling on the Spirit to make what he has begun in us mature and adult, because he knocks at our door, if we will let him in. Then He makes everything in us a cry to the Father and the power of the Father truly transforms us, and all this is the upheaval of our human categories (1 Corinthians 1-2).

ANOTHER THOUGHT MAKES itself felt in our meditation on the Ascension. Christ ascended into heaven: this is the eternal sign with which He spoke to the men of his time and to the whole world according to their mental capacities.

What does it mean for Christ to go up to heaven? It means that Christ, according to the story of salvation that the Father has established, entered into His definitive truth, or better still, into the accomplishment of His definitive truth.

The definitive truth of Christ is that He is the Lord of all things, in that all things consist in Him. Even if we do not see the "how," Christ is my consistence and your consistence; therefore the Ascension of Christ into heaven means that I am made of Christ, you are made of Christ, the flowers and the stars are made of Christ.

"All things came to be through him, and without him nothing came to be" (John 1:3): this, which has always been true for the Word, is the way with which the man-Christ, after his death and resurrection, possesses reality, and the Ascension into heaven is the definitiveness of this possession.

Heaven is not a "beyond" but is the ultimate level of things. So, to say that Christ ascended to heaven means saying that Christ descended into the depth of things.

Christ descended into the depth of our being and, because of this, rules us and constitutes us. The first consequence is that the mystery of the Ascension lives in us in the measure that conversion happens, which is the transformation and transfiguration of our way of being.

The transfiguration of our way of being demonstrates that Christ already possesses all things.

The total transfiguration will be at the end of the world, when Christ will appear as what He is: the ruler of all. But, in the measure that I live the conception of myself and of things according to Christ, in the faith and love of Christ, I anticipate, even in a shadowy way, this end of the world.

The Ascension is the mystery of the transfiguration of our actions and, therefore, is the mystery of daily life in so far as Christian reality shows itself as a human and earthly reality that has been changed and, therefore, as the accomplishment of the miracle.

"But grace was given to each of us according to the measure of Christ's gift. Therefore, it says: 'He ascended on high and took prisoners captive; he gave gifts to men'" (Ephesians 4:7-8).

Ascending on high, that is, accomplishing the truth of things that He himself is, Christ pulls behind himself a crowd of prisoners, that is, He frees even us. The Ascension is the feast of liberation, of daily transfiguration.

The thrust of our daily life is the mystery of Christ that takes possession of all things and knocks on our door, shakes our bed to wake us from sleep, and puts in our hands a different energy and a different sensibility into our heart: to recognize this is the transfiguration of our life.

It is the illumination of the way we look at ourselves and at everything around us, and therefore at our actions, because we realize the consistency that everything has in Christ.

With the Ascension the possibility of really transforming my life has begun. With the Ascension the real possibility of transforming the life of the world and the life of the Church has begun.

This beginning, which is already in me, proves itself, reveals itself, witnesses itself to my eyes and the eyes of the world the change in me. Thus the Ascension of Christ demonstrates that He is present through the new vibration that begins to unfold in us: the transfiguration of our actions.

"The one who descended is also the one who ascended far above all the heavens, that he might fill all things" (Ephesians 4:10).

The truth of the universe is Christ, and we are the ones for whom everyday life is the instrument with which we can fulfill our vocation: the vocation to fill the universe with Him; He fills the universe through us.

The Ascension is our true ethic, our true moral engagement, the description of the true dynamic of life. The true dynamic of life is the Ascension that is, in us, the outcome of the Resurrection of Christ: the transfiguration, the true face of things that begins to glimmer.

Chapter 6

PENTECOST

THE SPIRIT IS THE PRINCIPLE of seeing God, the principle of having an experience of God, the principle of the life of God in us and among us.

Pentecost makes clear what Jesus says in the Gospel of Saint John: "I came that they may have life. Now this is eternal life, that they should know you, the only true God, and the one whom you sent, Jesus Christ" (John 10:10; 17:3).

The Holy Spirit is the principle in us of the knowledge of the Father and the Son. The word knowledge in Christian language is much more vast and profound than the same term used according to the cultural tradition of the West (let's remember, for example, how the Bible, to talk about the relationship between man and woman, uses the term "knowledge").

The Holy Spirit is the principle of a real knowledge of the Father and the Son. This is something that is accomplished existentially. Knowledge happens by awakening an attention that presupposes attraction and brings with it sympathy. Therefore, it is full of love from its beginning.

In his last discourse, Jesus speaks about the Spirit.

> And I will ask the Father, and he will give you another Advocate to be with you always, the Spirit of truth, which the world cannot accept, because it neither sees nor knows it. But you know it, because it remains with you, and will be in you. I will not leave you orphans; I will

come to you. On that day you will realize that I am in my Father and you are in me and I in you. (John 14:16-18, 20)

"On that day you will realize that I am in the Father and you are in me and I in you." Here is the whole mystery of God in history. "He will teach you everything and remind you of all that I told you" (John 14:26).

"HE WILL TEACH YOU": this is not a superficial teaching, the purely notional teaching of human masters. "He will teach you that I am in the Father and you are in me and I in you": therefore the Holy Spirit, more than being a principle of the knowledge of the Father and the Son, and therefore the mystery of the relationship that exists between our person and the Creator, is also the principle of the knowledge of the mystery that determines the face of history and the world, the meaning of time: "This mystery was not made known to human beings in other generations as it has now been revealed to his holy apostles and prophets by the Spirit" (Ephesians 3:5).

The meaning of existence and of history was not revealed to the wise, nor to the philosophers, nor to the politicians, but to the holy apostles and prophets by means of the Spirit, whom Christ sent into the world, by means of the Spirit.

And my message and my proclamation were not with persuasive words of wisdom, but with a demonstration of spirit and power, so that your faith might rest not on human wisdom but on the power of God. (1 Corinthians 2:4-5)

The announcement, therefore, was not founded on theories, on arguments of human logic or human observations, but on the demonstration of spirit and power, on the newness of the experience that the Spirit raised up, on the miracle that the Spirit accomplished. Miracle: a change in the given experience, a change in the way of knowledge, of awareness; a change in the way of relating, a change in the feeling of the relationship and the energy of relationships. "We preach wisdom, but not the wisdom of this age, nor of the rulers of this world, that will be reduced to nothing. We preach the wisdom of God, a mysterious, a hidden wisdom and at the same time a demonstration of the Spirit and power" (1 Corinthians 2:4-7). This paradox is in us: the gift of a wisdom that God, before time began, had already destined for our glory, wisdom that none of the rulers of this world has ever known. If in fact they had known it, they would never have crucified the Lord of glory, but as Saint Paul wrote:

> "What eye has not seen, and ear has not heard, and what has not entered the human heart, what God has prepared for those who love him," this God has revealed to us through the Spirit. For the Spirit scrutinizes everything, even the depths of God. Among human beings, who knows what pertains to a person except the spirit of the person that is within? Similarly, no one knows what pertains to God except the Spirit of God. We have not received the spirit of the world but the Spirit that is from God, so that we may understand the things freely given us by God. And we speak about them not with words taught by human wisdom, but with words taught by the Spirit, describing spiritual realities in spiritual terms. Now the natural person does not accept what pertains to the Spirit of God, for to him it is foolishness, and he cannot understand it, because it is judged spiritually. The spiritual person, however, can judge everything but is not subject to judgment by anyone. For "who has known the mind of the Lord, so as to counsel him?" But we have the mind of Christ. (1 Corinthians 2:9-16)

The characteristic of the knowledge of the Father and the Son, of the mystery of the New Being that is in us and the mystery of history, is unmistakable: the *certainty* of possessing the Spirit of Christ.

What normally makes our experience a scandal in the eyes of others is instead the most beautiful symptom of its authenticity: certainty. A certainty that can remain, that subsists in the midst of aridity and in the midst even of temptation, in the midst of clouds and in the midst of the temptation to reject the faith.

"I speak the truth in Christ, I do not lie; my conscience joins with the holy Spirit in bearing me witness" (Romans 9:1). Certainly not a worldly certainty, which gives presumption, the worldly certainty of those who scrutinize the Scriptures like the Pharisees, who scrutinize the Scriptures with their head, or the certainty of those in the world who choose masters for themselves; not the certainty of those who lean on their own human measure, but the certainty that comes from the Spirit. The guarantee of this certainty is the faithfulness to the tradition of the Church; the verification of this certainty is time, the time of God's movement in history. As it was for the ancient Hebrews, the prophets, and the poor in spirit, the guarantee of certainty is the way God has acted in their history.

This meditation on the Spirit, who is the power with which Christ makes Himself present in history and therefore makes Himself in some way the content of an experience, consists in the first place in our affirmation that the Spirit is the principle of the knowledge of the Father and the Son, of the mystery that is in us, of the new being that is in us, and of the meaning of history.

THE SECOND STEP in this deepening comes from the word that Jesus uses in chapter 14 of the Gospel of St. John: "I will send you the Comforter" (John 14:16)—*Consolator optime*, the perfect comforter.

In order to understand well the idea, the light contained in this phrase, let us remember the words of Saint Paul: "to be strengthened with power through his Spirit in the inner self" (Ephesians 3:16).

Strengthened, *robur*, strength, energy: we are talking about the strength from on high (Luke 24:40) which the Acts of the Apostles calls the Spirit. The strength from on high, and "high" means deep.

Strengthened, made strong within, a strength that is given to us from within. But when do we feel comforted? We feel comforted by the content of an experience; we feel comforted by the content of an event, by something that happens. An event, interior or exterior, raises us up, lifts our hearts, fills our life again, raises up our person to the point of filling us with joy. Joy is born in this new strength, in the lifting up of the heart, in this energy that forms within us.

Joy is made possible, happiness and joy.

If we want to use an analogy from religious experience for a phenomenon that happens so many times, we can refer to when we encounter a person, receive a phone call, a letter, and then we are changed from within, we are no longer how we were an hour or a day earlier. If we want to use an analogy that is a little farther away, we could say: it is a miracle, because the miracle is the event of life, of perfection, of holiness, the event of the revival of life, the event of creation. We would use the word miracle.

The Holy Spirit is in us the principle of this miracle for which our life is full of consolation, of comfort. This does not happen directly, but something that changes provokes consolation and comfort in us. All this belongs to what Saint Paul in the first letter to the Corinthians called "a demonstration of spirit and power" (2:4). We remember, in fact, that, in the beginning, the descent of the Spirit on the person who was baptized, the communication of the Spirit that made one a Christian, was demonstrated with sensible wonders.

Christian life is totally sustained by this demonstration of the Spirit and power, and therefore Christian life is filled with consolation and comfort.

This is the intervention and the prophecy of the intervention of God in history and in the world because, according to the human measure, there is no change, only a formal, and therefore illusory, game. The Holy Spirit is not only the knowledge that ignites the life of the new being in us and of the true meaning of existence and history but is already the pledge, the deposit, the beginning of a change, the beginning of a change in our existence, the beginning of a change that is the content of an experience.

Our life is, through the Spirit that is in us, a road of changes, or the road of change, the road of transfiguration, or better, the road of resurrection. And precisely the recognition of this confirms us, makes us strong, consoles us.

"But the one who gives us security with you in Christ and who anointed us is God; he has also put his seal upon us and given the Spirit in our hearts as a first installment" (2 Corinthians 1:21-22).

"He has also put his seal upon us": this word in Christian language means a change of being (what the Catechism calls *character*). This seal is a new face, that is, a new being.

"He has put his seal upon us and given the Spirit in our hearts." Heart is the fullness of knowledge. It is the feeling and passion for life, full of intelligence and will. The heart is the principle of life as experience, of the experience of life, of the experimentality of life, of the passion of life. "The pledge of the Spirit": this means something that will be given but that is already given now. What will be given to us? The complete manifestation of our perfection will be given to us in the final resurrection; but it has already begun, through the pledge of the Spirit, the gift of change. Christian history, Christian existence, is the story of a change, of the Resurrection that confirms itself, not abstractly, but in the "I" that changes in knowledge and consolation.

So let us examine two fruits of this consolation, of this comforting change, two elements of this new experience of life.

The first is indicated in Romans 8:15-16: "For you did not receive a spirit of slavery to fall back into fear, but you received a spirit of adoption, through which we cry, 'Abba, Father!' The Spirit itself bears witness with our spirit that we are children of God." The Spirit gives witness that we are children of God. "As proof that you are children, God sent the spirit of his Son into our hearts, crying out, 'Abba, Father!'" (Galatians 4:6).

The Spirit of the Son cries out in us: Abba, Father! It is a change: I am no longer I.

"And no one can say, 'Jesus is Lord,' except by the Holy Spirit" (1 Corinthians 12:3). The Spirit is the power with which Christ makes himself present. In fact, if we say Lord or Jesus, it means that another power makes us capable of saying it, because we cannot give faith to ourselves, the knowledge and sense of faith do not belong to us.

So what is the supreme expression of this first fruit of the Spirit in us, that gives us knowledge and consolation? The first fruit of this consolation is the capacity to say "Father" to God that only we can have. No one can say "Father" to God like we can.

The second fruit of the Spirit is hope. The new figure that the Spirit creates in the world is, in a certain way, physically visible: the figure of the Christian, *spe erectus*, standing upright in hope.

"May the God of hope fill you with all joy and peace in believing, so that you may abound in hope by the power of the holy Spirit" (Romans 15:13).

"That you may abound in hope"; "the God of hope." But we cannot understand the word hope if we do not quickly affirm that this implies a past, because hope is first of all the fulfillment of a promise. The fulfillment of a promise, the realization of the Covenant. Therefore, Saint Paul in the Letter to the Ephesians calls the Spirit, "the Spirit of the promise" (Vulgate, *Spiritus promissionis*).

"Sealed with the promised holy Spirit" (Ephesians 1:13).

The promises are the promised Spirit: the Spirit who generates new life, the new creation, *Creator Spiritus*.

Saint James says, "He willed to give us birth by the word of truth that we may be a kind of first fruits of his creatures" (James 1:18), of his new creation.

"Sealed with the promised Holy Spirit." He is the pledge of an experience. He is the beginning of the final experience, the beginning of the experience of Paradise.

On the basis of this, Saint Paul could say, "We even boast of our afflictions" (Romans 5:3), and even Saint Therese of the Child Jesus could underline at the end of her life, when temptation made it seem to her that she had lost her faith: "We even boast of our afflictions." It is paradoxical, because the certainty of the Spirit remains. "He is the first installment of our inheritance" (Ephesians 1:14).

"For through the Spirit, by faith, we await the hope of righteousness" (Galatians 5:5). What is righteousness?

Righteousness, or justice, is the story of God in the world. It is the meaning of the events of God in the world.

Through the Spirit we await the hope that justice inspires in us. Pay attention: it is "another us" who hopes in us!

We hope for the fulfillment of a promise, but this promise is not a word that was spoken to us. It is a fact that happened in us.

The Spirit, this power that has recreated us, that has made us new beings and that is the beginning of a new experience, that makes us pray to the Father, that gives hope to our life, is exactly the opposite of the concept of worldly hope.

In fact, worldly hope is uncertainty; here instead it is life that becomes ever more certain, that is, hope in so far as it is the expectation of something whose beginning I already have in my hands, the pledge and deposit. The Covenant, the contract that was made, the engagement, is already here; the end has already begun.

This Spirit comes to us from the cross of Christ because that is the event in which the deposit, the pledge was won for us.

This Spirit cannot be illusory, cannot be a stand-in for our feelings. He is the Spirit of Christ, that comes from the cross of Christ, from the resurrection of Christ, and from the law of Christ in history, which is the Church.

"For neither does circumcision mean anything, nor does uncircumcision, but only a new creation. Peace and mercy be to all who follow this rule and to the Israel of God" (Galatians 6:15-16). Peace and mercy on the person and on the people: these are the fruit of hope.

IN CONCLUSION, WE cannot but recall Saint Paul again: "Do you not know that you are not your own?" (1 Corinthians 6:19). We are not our own, I am not my own, I do not belong to myself, my person is not mine, "I live, no longer I, but Christ lives in me" (Galatians 2:20).

This is really a new being that is born from our humanity and from the Spirit that is in us, and everything stretches toward the moment when the glorified body will also appear transfigured by the Spirit that was already in us and that already gave indications of His presence, the principle of the experience of God, of God's making himself an experience and of the fact that we do not belong to ourselves.

> As indeed he says in Hosea: "Those who were not my people I will call 'my people,' and her who was not beloved I will call 'beloved.' And in the very place where it was said to them, 'You are not my people,' there they shall be called children of the living God." (Romans 9:25-26)

My people, children of the living God, delight, "you belong to me," we do not belong to ourselves: that which is not His people, this flesh and this spirit, this humanity that is not His, but that is at the mercy of a lie, *becomes* His. It is precisely in the place where it is said "You are not mine" that this humanity of ours—whose measure tends to oppose itself to God—it is right here, in this measure of our mind, this feeling of our heart, these instincts of our body, this experience of ours, that *becomes* the place where we feel ourselves echoing the words "child of the living God, my delight, my people." The experience of man, the horizon of human experience—the place where man tends to affirm his self-love, his own measure, and is consequently a place full of fear, if not of presumption—it is precisely in this place that man hears himself echoing: "my people, my delight, child of the living God."

We begin to feel our belonging to God.

Chapter 7

TRINITY

THE LITURGY OF THE Most Holy Trinity is the fundamental meditation, the alpha and omega of everything.

It is a hidden mystery even if it has been revealed; it is the foundation that we will never be able to exhaust, not even in eternity, when we will see Him face to face.

From the Epistle of Saint Paul to the Corinthians: "The grace of the Lord Jesus Christ and the love of God and the fellowship of the Holy Spirit be with all of you" (2 Corinthians 13:13).

The word "grace" summarizes, to the fullest extent of its meaning, what God is for us: that is, everything.

The Trinity is the source of grace, from our origin to our eternal destiny, from our nature which is constructed to receive sonship with God, and thus likeness with Christ, from the mysterious embryonic beginning of history to its eternal expansion. Grace is the origin of everything.

The idea that most clearly enhances this word, so open and clear in its immediate sense as it is mysterious in the interior root of its meaning, is made explicit by the concept of "Covenant": the old and the new Covenant.

Already in the chapters of Genesis, in the story of Abraham, the Covenant refers to a design that God establishes, calling man as an actor in this design. And what God begins He brings to completion.

The word grace coincides as a metaphor—the most suitable that God has revealed in the long story of the people of Israel, in our education to whom Christ is the definitive step—with the word "rock."

The word grace that dominates the brief epistle in the Mass for the Trinity[15] is the rock on which our life is founded, on which our life is built; but it is a certainty, an absolute security that moves forward in our soul, because God is faithful.

Our rejection of God—not just occasionally but frequently—our irreligiosity, our true rebellion against God, can only amount to one thing: a lack of belief that what God has started He will bring to completion.

The first value for us of the Trinity is this immense rock on which we are founded, on which we have been grafted, and that will never wear away. God is not first of all faithful to us; God is faithful to Himself, and therefore, if He has begun something in us, being faithful to Himself, He is faithful to the end. The true irreligiosity, the true rebellion against God, is to found our certainty, our faithfulness, and to seek our salvation in something other than this rock.

The Trinity is the mystery of security, the mystery of certainty.

Security and certainty not because I decided to be faithful but because He is faithful to Himself: security and certainty build on the historical fact that God has loved us. Our wealth is this security. Our certainty is the fact of God. There is no other thought that can allow us and reanimate us to choose the good in any situation as if it were the beginning. There is no other thought that can give us newness of life like this.

THE SECOND ASPECT OF this mystery, underlined above all from the Gospel of the octave of Pentecost (see John 15:26-16:4, again in the pre-Vatican II Ambrosian Missal), is that *the Holy Spirit makes us understand what God is for us and also what we are for Him*.

This second aspect is *charity*. Charity is this great divesting of self, this recognition of our own nothingness by which my consistency is an Other. Recognition that is translated dynamically, that is, ethically, with the fact that His will is my will, that the law of my action is an Other, and therefore everything in me is obedience. It is obedience, or more concretely still and more simply, imitation. In any case, it is charity.

And this has as a corollary the humanly impossible fact by which others become a part of me, by which we are all one thing with those that God has called. Conversion is to recognize this and make it the practice of our life.

We cannot think about the Trinity without all of our barriers falling, at least in principle, in front of the fact of this unity. Barriers that are very easy to understand, because the barriers are always reactions. Reactions that get summed up in the word personalism or individualism (but the word personalism masks even more the pretense, our attempts to justify our own individualism).

To live the mystery of the Trinity is not the renunciation of our own personality. In fact, the personality of each person of the Trinity is such in so far as they are together. So true is this that in theology the Persons are called relations, "subsistent relations." This is the paradox, that the infinitely unmistakable personality— the personality of the Father, the Son, and the Holy Spirit—"is" because they are together, because they are in relationship. This is the foundation of the value of the personality, and only Christian discourse clarifies it to this point.

Grace is not something as abstract as we might think when we study theology. His grace is an historical communication, an historical fact in our life.

Let us meditate in the first place on the security of God. If we found our security on grace, we could not help but produce fruit; by its nature grace pulls us out of our inertia and saves us. It pulls us out of our nothingness and saves us from sin—the nothingness of inertia, of the futile and arid wandering of instinctiveness—and from evil as the attempt to return to nothing, that is, to that inertia. This is our inactivity or rigidity, like a glacier, the hardening and numbness that we suffer, because we are not supported by grace, by the word of the epistle for today, which is that the Trinity is origin, master, *Dominus*. This is our security: that He is Lord.

In the second place, let us reflect on observing His commandments, that is, on imitation. Otherwise, the observation of His commandments would mean only not sinning, which is one aspect of the question; but if it is not a dynamic aspect, it is Pharisaical, limiting, a denial: to observe his commandments means imitation, obedience.

Obedience means that there is something that calls us and toward which we must reach out. We do not adhere to our vocation if we are not stretched toward this obedience. "If you love me, you will keep my commandments" (John 14:15). His commandments are not laws per se, but are rather an invitation to what is paradigmatic in Jesus Christ.

Appendix 1

NOTE ON THE FIRST EDITION OF 1973

WE HAVE TITLED THESE brief notes a "witness" because we believe that, even with the inadequacy of summarizing and transcribing oral discourse, we can still retrace in this text the fundamentals for understanding the place occupied by our commitment to living the liturgy in the life of the movement founded by Father Giussani, Communion and Liberation.

The liturgy is an indicator of fundamental importance for becoming aware of how any manifestation of Christian communion lives and understands itself in the Church. And it is so much more important because in our time the liturgy is generally neglected as a gauge of communion. If we want to understand what conception of the Church animates a group, a community, a movement, today we tend to consider above all the aspects of intervention on the great problems current in the Church, on opinions expressed, on the activities it supports or its opposition to certain topics, considered as foundational. All this clearly has its value but can hide a defacement, a duality in our understanding of the Church, which distinguishes itself only when it questions itself about the nexus that links every possible intervention and engagement in social and ecclesial life to the rhythms with which the Church herself lives the mystery in the world.

Hamman says in the introduction to his text *Liturgical and Social Life*: "The diversity of tasks in the Church risks hiding their solidarity and unity. To some contemplation, to others action; to the priests spiritual responsibility, to the laity temporal duties! Everyone is jealous for his specialty and his autonomy. Each consecrates himself to a liturgy that does not lead to a committed life, others exhaust themselves in civic and social action, but because the evangelical roots are lacking, they cease to be a witness."

The truly revelatory point of the liturgy is how much it is able to be the "root" of Christian life, a root that gives life to the tree, the flowers, the fruits in the providential fact of its growth.

These notes were taken in the course of conversations that sought to teach something fundamental: the mystery of the liturgical life is the paradigm of life, an occasion of encounter with the Presence that saves the world and that, if it is accepted as such, cannot be lived in a context that relegates it to a moment of spiritual rest, however comforting, but does not impact one's life and personality.

The insistence on this teaching is so much more notable if we think that these notes were chosen in the arc of numerous dialogues that cover a period from 1965 to 1973.

We have selected some points from which it seemed sufficiently clear how we attempted to connect the awareness of the one who listens to the fact of Christian commitment with the totality of its implications.

Such totality is so inconspicuous that the Christian can hear it re-proposed for years, forget it, and continue to rediscover it with the intuition that always emerges when facing something new. The Church shows her wisdom in this continual proposal of the mystery as a factor in our life, and through these notes it seems we can glimpse how a life of Christian communion can learn from this wisdom a method that is so radically consonant with the person, who, in ignorance of their humanity, they would never have known to invent.

—Milan, 1973

Appendix 2

CURATOR'S NOTE

THE BOOK YOU HAVE before you re-proposes the text in its original version, from 1973, with the title *From the Lived Liturgy: A Testimony. Notes taken in the course of community conversations, redacted by Maretta Campi*, with errors corrected and sections omitted from the preceding editions and with a new set of notes for the numerous biblical references, originally presented in parentheses within the text. Annotations have been added to help the contemporary reader with some context for the period 1965-1973, during which these lessons were given by Father Giussani and upon which these texts were derived, a time marked by the progressive implementation of the liturgical reform of the Second Vatican Council, which also, especially in the Diocese of Milan, had a unique form, due to adapting the Ambrosian Rite to the modifications introduced in the Roman Rite.

It is also helpful to remember that the first edition of the Bible in the Italian language edited by the Italian Bishops Conference, which was then made "official" by its liturgical use, was published in 1971, while as regards the euchological texts (that is to say, the fixed and moveable liturgical texts of the eucharistic liturgy), the Ordinary of the Mass in Italian came out in 1969, the complete Missal in 1973 for the Roman Rite, and in 1976 for the Ambrosian Rite. It is not surprising, therefore, that in the meditations of Father Giussani we find biblical citations—belonging to Italian translations that precede 1971—that sound somewhat different than those more recognizable to us, together with comments on liturgical texts that touch both the celebration before Vatican II (what today is called the "extraordinary form" of the Roman or Ambrosian Rite) and the post-conciliar version (the so-called "Missal of Paul VI"). In particular, as regards the Ordinary of the Mass, Father Giussani sometimes refers to texts carried over faithfully to the edition of 1969 but which still underwent changes in the successive complete editions of the Roman and Ambrosian Missals.

The redactional choices—coming from the desire to respect as much as possible the original text—make note of the more evident textual discrepancies, also highlighting the correct biblical references for scriptural passages and the sources of liturgical texts.

Even this aspect, however, is not only a technical detail, because these notes allow us to highlight the content and the method chosen by Father Giussani: the teachings here proposed, in fact, are placed, because of their radicality in discussing in depth the meaning of the liturgy, above the debate (at times quite bitter) about the post-Conciliar reforms, and offer texts and reflections that, tapping into the theological-liturgical patrimony before and after Vatican II, are perfectly valuable at the present time. The current circumstance, then, in which celebrations according to the pre-Conciliar liturgical form are taking place again, can also allow those who prefer this ritual form to find in this volume a solid and consistent nourishment for their own journey of faith.

Francesco Braschi

NOTES

1. This canticle is also found in the Liturgy of the Hours of both the Roman and the Ambrosian Rite, at lauds of the first Friday of the Psalter.

2. A.N. Whitehead, *Religion in the Making* (Harvard, 1926), 16.

3. Cf. Sirach 18:23 in the Vulgate: "Ante orationem praepara animam tuam et noli esse quasi homo qui temptat Deum."

4. This is the conclusion of the profession of faith in the Rite of Baptism.

5. Rite of Mass, prayer of the celebrant before washing hands.

6. Rite of Mass, presentation of the gifts.

7. Rite of Mass, Eucharistic prayer II.

8. Rite of Mass, Eucharistic prayer II.

9. Rite of Mass, prayer after Our Father.

10. Rite of Mass, invitation to exchange peace before Communion.

11. Rite of Mass: Eucharistic Prayer II.

12. St. John of the Cross, *Dichos* 64.

13. This passage from the Gospel of John comes from the Third Sunday of Lent in the Ambrosian Rite, which is called "Abraham Sunday." Along with the references to the Samaritan woman, the man born blind, and Lazarus, Giussani refers to the Lenten Sundays as they are celebrated in the liturgy of the Church of Milan.

14. Here is a reference to the Christmas hymn by Saint Ambrose, *Illuminans altissimus*, which, echoing Psalm 19:6 in the Latin text, defines the sun, and thus the Word of God, as "geminae gigas substantiae / alacris ut currat viam [giant of twin substance / swift to run its way]."

15. The single verse cited above (2 Corinthians 13:13) constitutes the Epistle of the Feast of the Holy Trinity in the Ambrosian Missal in use before the Second Vatican Council, until 1976.

This book was set in Adobe Caslon Pro, designed by Carol Twombly and released in 1990. The typeface is named after the British typefounder William Caslon (1692-1766) and grew out of Twombly's study of Caslon's specimen sheets. Though Caslon began his career making "exotic" typefaces—Hebrew, Arabic, and Coptic—his Roman typeface became the standard for text printed in English for most of the eighteenth century, including the Declaration of Independence.

This book was designed by Shannon Carter, Ian Creeger, and Gregory Wolfe. It was published in hardcover, paperback, and electronic formats by Slant Books, Seattle, Washington.

Cover photograph by Francesco Alberti: Seminario inferiore, Venegono, Italy, via Unsplash.

Milton Keynes UK
Ingram Content Group UK Ltd.
UKHW011023250224
438207UK00011BA/71/J